7-DAY AFGHANS

Jean Leinhauser & Rita Weiss

Sterling Publishing Co., Inc.   New York

*We have made every effort to ensure the accuracy and
completeness of the instructions in this book.
We cannot, however, be responsible for human error,
typographical mistakes or variations in individual work.*

*Book Design by CBG Graphics, Hartsdale, New York
Carol Belanger Grafton, Designer*

Copyright © 1985 by Jean Leinhauser and Rita Weiss
Published by Sterling Publishing Co., Inc.
387 Park Avenue South, New York, N.Y. 10016
First published in hardcover under the
title, "The 7-Day Afghan Book"
Distributed in Canada by Sterling Publishing
℅ Canadian Manda Group, P.O. Box 920, Station U
Toronto, Ontario, Canada M8Z 5P9
Manufactured in the United States of America
All rights reserved
Sterling ISBN 0-8069-5709-3 Paper

INTRODUCTION

In today's busy world, time is at a premium. Knitters are still knitting, and crocheters are still crocheting; but now they are looking for projects that are quick and easy to make—yet look just as wonderful as the more complex old designs.

This book is designed to provide a wealth of afghans that are not only beautiful, but easy, fun *and* fast to make.

Most of them are made with big needles or hooks, some with two strands of yarn. The patterns are easy to follow and represent a wonderful variety of stitches and textures.

The afghans can be made in a week—but that, of course, depends on how many hours a day you're planning to spend with your crochet hook or your knitting needles, and how fast you work.

We'd like to stress that knitting and crocheting are not a race—there's no prize for the one who gets there first! Take the time to enjoy your work, to relax, to have fun. Don't feel you're up against the clock or the calendar just because we called this **7-DAY AFGHANS.**

We've tried to include just about every kind of afghan you could want: granny squares, ripples, fisherman, cables; traditional patterns and colors, as well as bright and bold modern designs; plus a special selection of patterns that everyone loves to make—baby afghans.

We hope you'll have many hours of pleasure making these afghans.

1455 Linda Vista
San Marcos, CA 92069

Jean Leinhauser
Rita Weiss

DEDICATION

This book is dedicated to Barbara Hunter of Prescott Valley, AZ, who designed many of the afghans and organized a hard-working and talented crew of knitters and crocheters to produce the models in record time. Teacher, author, designer, and outstanding needlewoman, Barbara has also been a dear and cherished friend for many years.

ACKNOWLEDGMENTS

AMERICAN THREAD kindly permitted us to use a number of designs which we originally created for them in Dawn Sayelle* worsted weight yarn.

CARON INTERNATIONAL provided us with four original afghan designs, and donated many skeins of their Dazzleaire worsted weight yarn.

COATS & CLARK generously provided several afghan designs, and the color photographs of the finished projects.

AMERICAN SCHOOL OF NEEDLEWORK, INC. let us use a number of designs and photographs from their books.

Gayle Motsinger of **GAYLEMOT PUBLISHING** not only permitted us to use several designs and photographs from her books, but let us disrupt her business for two days while we photographed in her studio.

And finally, our special thanks go to **Carol Wilson Mansfield,** who directed all of the original photography done for this book.

CONTENTS

Chapter 6: BABY QUICKIES to Knit & Crochet   119

INDEX   144

AFGHAN TECHNIQUES

To make your afghaning go more quickly and be more fun, we've included here a complete "refresher course" on the knit and crochet techniques required.

We suggest that you read this section, hook or needles handy, and work through any steps that are unfamiliar to you. There are a number of special techniques that you may not have done before, and be sure to try those.

You certainly don't have to be an expert to make our quick afghans, but you'll enjoy it more if you're sure of what you're doing.

KNITTING

CASTING ON (CO)

Only one knitting needle is used with this method. First, measure off a length of yarn that allows about 1″ for each stitch you are going to cast on. Make a slip knot on needle as follows. Make a yarn loop, leaving about 4″ length of yarn at free end; insert needle into loop and draw up yarn from free end to make a loop on needle (**Fig 1**). Pull yarn firmly, but not tightly, to form a slip knot on needle (**Fig 2**). This slip knot counts as your first stitch. Now work as follows.

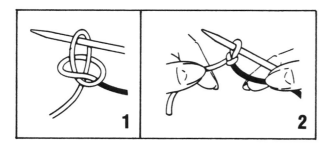

Step 1: Hold needle with slip knot in right hand, with yarn from skein to your right, and measured length of yarn to your left. With left hand, make a yarn loop (**Fig 3** and insert needle into loop (**Fig 4**).

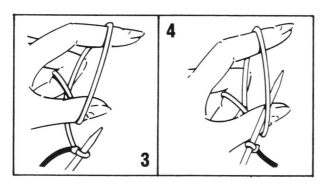

Step 2: Still holding loop in left hand, with right hand, pick up yarn from skein and bring it from back to front around the needle (**Fig 5**).

Step 3: Bring needle through loop and toward you; at the same time, pull gently on yarn end to tighten loop (**Fig 6**). Make it snug but not tight below needle.

You now have one cast-on stitch. Repeat Steps 1 through 3 for each additional stitch desired.

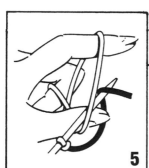

THE KNIT STITCH (K)

Step 1: Hold the needle with cast-on stitches in your left hand. Insert point of right needle in first stitch, from left to right, just as in casting on (**Fig 7**).

Step 2: With right index finger, bring yarn under and over point of right needle (**Fig 8**).

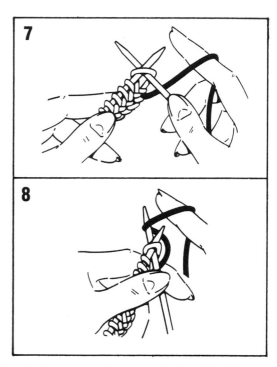

Step 3: Draw yarn through stitch with right needle point (**Fig 9**).

Step 4: Slip the loop on the left needle off, so the new stitch is entirely on the right needle (**Fig 10**).

This completes one knit stitch.

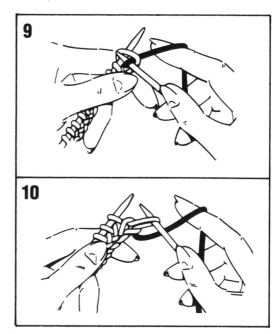

THE PURL STITCH (P)

The reverse of the knit stitch is called the purl stitch. Instead of inserting the right needle point from left to right under the left needle (as you did for the knit stitch), you will now insert it from right to left, in front of the left needle.

Step 1: Insert right needle, from right to left, into first stitch, and in front of left needle (**Fig 11**).

Step 2: Holding yarn in front of work (side toward you), bring it around right needle counterclockwise (**Fig 12**).

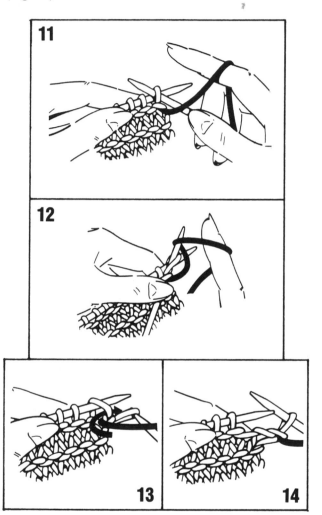

Step 3: With right needle, pull yarn back through stitch (**Fig 13**). Slide stitch off left needle, leaving new stitch on right needle (**Fig 14**).

One purl stitch is now completed.

BINDING OFF (BO)

To bind off on the knit side:

Step 1: Knit the first 2 stitches. Then insert left needle into the first of the 2 stitches (**Fig 15**), and pull it over the second stitch and completely off the needle (**Fig 16**). You have now bound off one stitch.

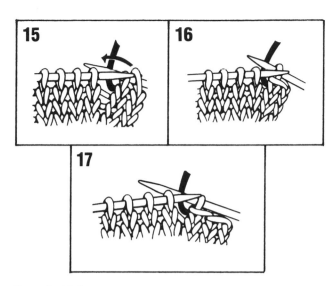

Step 2: Knit one more stitch; insert left needle into first stitch on right needle and pull it over the new stitch and completely off the needle (**Fig 17**). Another stitch is now bound off.

Repeat Step 2 until all sts are bound off and one loop remains on right-hand needle. "Finish off" or "end off" the yarn (cut yarn and draw end through last loop).

To bind off on the purl side:

Step 1: Purl the first 2 stitches. Now insert left needle into the first stitch on right needle, and pull it over the second stitch and completely off the needle. You have now bound off one stitch.

Step 2: Purl one more stitch; insert left needle into first stitch on right needle and pull it over the new stitch and completely off the needle. Another stitch is bound off.

Repeat Step 2 until all sts are bound off.

YARN OVER (YO)

To make a yarn over before a knit stitch, bring yarn to front of work as if you were going to purl, then take it over the right needle to the back into the position for knitting; then knit the next stitch (**Fig 18**).

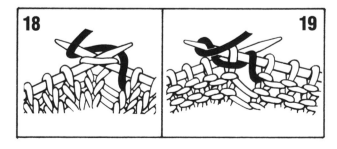

To make a yarn over before a purl stitch, bring yarn around right needle from front to back, then back around into position for purling; purl the next stitch (**Fig 19**).

INCREASING

Increasing is a shaping technique in which stitches are added, making the knitted piece wider. The most commonly used method to work an increase is to knit (or purl) twice into the same stitch. Another method is called "yarn over," and is used for a decorative increase as in a raglan seam, and for lacy, openwork patterns.

NOTE

Use this method only when specified in pattern instructions, as it leaves a small hole in your work.

Knit 2 Stitches in One. Step 1: Insert tip of right needle into stitch from front to back as to knit; now knit the stitch in the usual manner but don't remove the stitch from the left needle (**Fig 20**).

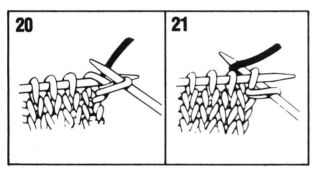

Step 2: Insert right needle (from front to back) into **back** loop of **same** stitch, and knit it again (**Fig 21**), this time slipping the stitch off the left needle. *You have now increased one stitch.*

Purl 2 Stitches in One. Step 1: Insert right needle into stitch from back to front as to purl; now purl the stitch in the usual manner but don't remove the stitch from the left needle.

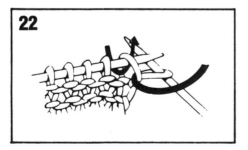

Step 2: Insert right needle (from back to front) into **back** loop of **same** stitch (**Fig 22**) and purl it again, this time slipping the stitch off the left needle. *You have now increased one stitch.*

Yarn Over (between 2 knit stitches): Bring yarn to **front** of work as if you were going to purl, then take it **over** the right needle to **back** of work. Yarn is now in position to knit the next stitch (**Fig 23**). *You have added one stitch.*

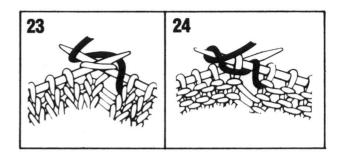

Yarn Over (between 2 purl stitches): Bring yarn **over** right needle to **back** of work, then bring yarn forward between the needles to **front** of work. Yarn is now in position to purl the next stitch (**Fig 24**). *You have added one stitch.*

DECREASING

Another shaping technique is decreasing, in which stitches are taken off, making the knitted piece narrower. These two methods of decreasing are most often used in knitting.

Knit (or purl) 2 Stitches Together: This method, abbreviated K2 tog (P2 tog), is worked simply by knitting (or purling) 2 stitches as one.

To work **K2 tog,** insert right needle through the fronts of first 2 stitches on left needle as to knit (**Fig 25**), then knit these 2 stitches as one (**Fig 26**). *You have decreased one stitch.*

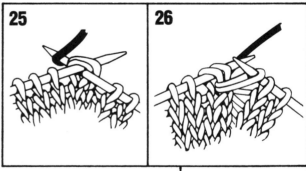

To work **P2 tog,** insert right needle through the fronts of next 2 stitches on left needle as to purl (**Fig 27**), then purl these 2 stitches as one. *You have decreased one stitch.*

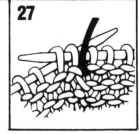

Pass Slipped Stitch Over: This method, abbreviated PSSO, is often used in the shaping of raglans or other pieces where a definite decrease line is desired. To use this method you must first know how to **"slip" a stitch,** which is an action that transfers a stitch from the left needle to the right needle without working it.

"Slip a stitch as to knit" is used when decreasing. To do this, insert right needle into stitch on left needle as if you were going to knit it; but instead of knitting, slip the stitch from left needle to right needle (*Fig 28*).

"Slip a stitch as to purl" is used when working a pattern stitch, so that on the next row of the pattern, the slipped stitch will be on the needle in the correct position for knitting (or purling). To do this, insert right needle into stitch on left needle as if you were going to purl it; but instead of purling, slip the stitch from left needle to right needle (*Fig 29*).

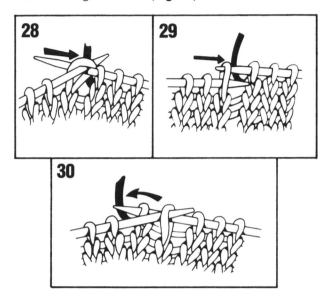

Now that you know how to slip a stitch, you can practice the second method of decreasing.

To work PSSO, slip the next stitch as to knit, then knit the next stitch, now pass the slipped stitch **over** the knitted stitch by using the point of the left needle to lift the slipped stitch over the knitted stitch as in binding off (*Fig 30*).

JOINING YARN

New yarn should be added only at the **beginning** of a row, never in the middle of a row, unless this is required for a color pattern change. To add yarn, tie the new strand around the old strand, making a knot at the edge of work (*Fig 31*), leaving at least a 4" end on both old and new strands.

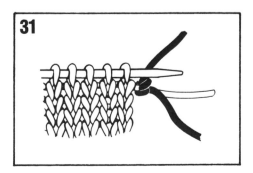

GAUGE AND MEASURING

Gauge simply means the number of stitches per inch, and the number of rows per inch, that result from a specified yarn worked with needles in a specified size. But since everyone knits differently—some loosely, some tightly, some in between—the measurements of individual work will vary greatly, even when the knitters use the exact same pattern and the exact same size yarn and needles.

Needle sizes given in instructions are merely guides, and should never be used without making a 4" square sample swatch to check your gauge. It is your responsibility to make sure you achieve the gauge specified in the pattern.

To achieve the gauge specified, you may need to use a different needle size—either larger or smaller—than that specified in the pattern. If you have more stitches or rows per inch than specified, you will have to try a size larger needles. If you have fewer stitches or rows per inch than specified, you will have to try a size smaller needles. ***Do not hesitate to change to larger or smaller needles if necessary to achieve gauge.***

WEAVING IN ENDS

When you finish your afghan, weave in all the yarn ends securely. To do this, use a size 16 tapestry needle, or a plastic yarn needle, and weave the yarn end through the backs of stitches (*Fig 32*), first weaving about 2" in one direction and then 1" in the reverse direction. Cut off excess yarn.

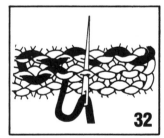

NOTE
Never weave in more than one yarn end at a time.

CORRECTING MISTAKES

Dropped Stitches: Each time you knit or purl a stitch, take care to pull the stitch off the left needle after completing the new stitch. Otherwise, you will be adding stitches when you don't want to. Don't let a stitch slip off the needle **before** you've knitted or purled it—that's called a **dropped stitch.** Even expert knitters drop a stitch now and then, but it's easy to pick up when you know how. A dropped stitch can be picked up several rows after it has been dropped by using a crochet hook.

To **pick up** a dropped stitch, have the knit side (right side of work) facing you. Insert the crochet hook into the dropped stitch from front to back, under the horizontal strand in the row above (**Fig 33**). Hook the horizontal strand above and pull through the loop on the crochet hook. Continue in this manner up to the working row, then transfer the loop from the crochet hook to the left needle, being careful not to twist it (**Fig 34**).

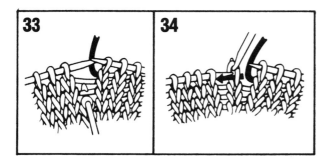

Unraveling Stitches: Sometimes it is necessary to unravel a large number of stitches, even down several rows, to correct a mistake. Whenever possible, carefully unravel the stitches one-by-one by putting the needle into the row below (**Fig 35**) and undoing the stitch above, until the mistake is reached.

If several rows need to be unraveled, carefully slide all stitches off the needle and unravel each row down to the row in which the error occurred. Then unravel this row, stitch by stitch, placing each stitch back on the needle in the correct position, without twisting it.

FOR LEFT HANDERS...

Many left-handed people learn to knit by reversing the stitches—a method we do not recommend. Instead, we suggest lefties try the Continental Method, in which the left hand does more of the work than the right.

Here is how to work in the Continental Method:

Knitting: Hold yarn in left hand, over index finger, as in **Fig 36.**

Step 1: Insert point of right needle into front of stitch on left needle as to knit.

Step 2: Catch yarn with point of right needle and draw yarn through (**Fig 37**), making a new loop.

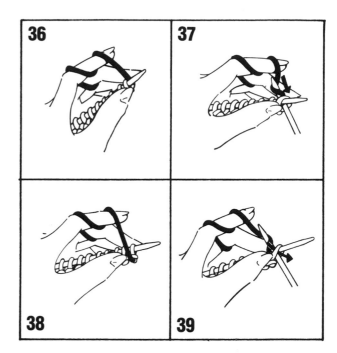

Step 3: Slip stitch off left needle: one knit stitch made. Repeat Steps 1 through 3 across row.

Purling: Hold yarn in left hand, over index finger, in front of work (**Fig 38**).

Step 1: Insert point of right needle into front of stitch on left needle as to purl, keeping it behind yarn on left index finger.

Step 2: Catch yarn around point of right needle (**Fig 39**) and draw yarn backward and up through stitch, making a new loop.

Step 3: Slip stitch off left needle: one purl stitch made. Repeat Steps 1 through 3 across row.

CROCHETING

CHAIN (ch)

Crochet always starts with a basic chain. To begin, make a slip loop on hook (**Fig 40**), leaving a 4" tail of yarn.

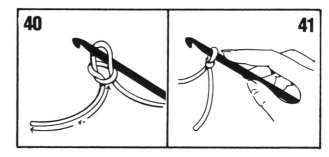

Step 1: Take a hook in right hand, holding it between thumb and third finger (**Fig 41**), and rest index finger near tip of hook.

Step 2: Take slip loop in thumb and index finger of left hand (**Fig 42**) and bring yarn over third finger of left hand, catching it loosely at left palm with remaining two fingers.

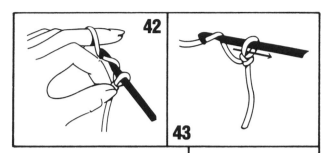

Step 3: Bring yarn over hook from back to front (**Fig 43**), and draw through loop on hook.

One chain made. Repeat Step 3 for each additional chain desired, moving your left thumb and index finger up close to the hook after each stitch or two (**Fig 44**).

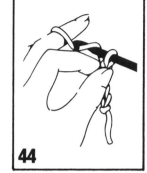

When counting number of chains, do not count the loop on the hook or the starting slip knot.

SINGLE CROCHET (sc)

First, make a chain to desired length.

Step 1: Insert hook in top loop of 2nd chain from hook (**Fig 45**); hook yarn (bring yarn over hook from back to front) and draw through (**Fig 46**).

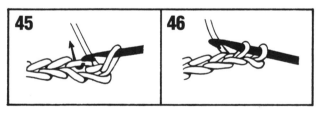

Step 2: Hook yarn and draw through 2 loops on hook (**Fig 47**).

One single crochet made. Work a single crochet (repeat Steps 1 and 2) in each remaining chain.

To work additional rows, chain 1 and turn work counterclockwise. Inserting hook under 2 top loops of the stitch (**Fig 48**), work a single crochet (as before) in each stitch across.

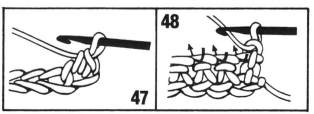

DOUBLE CROCHET (dc)

Double crochet is a taller stitch than single crochet. Begin by making a chain to desired length.

Step 1: Bring yarn once over the hook; insert hook in the top loop of the 4th chain from hook (**Fig 49**). Hook yarn and draw through (**Fig 50**).

Step 2: Hook yarn and draw through first 2 loops on hook (**Fig 51**).

Step 3: Hook yarn and draw through last 2 loops on hook (**Fig 52**).

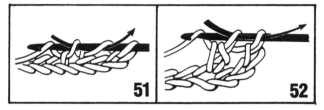

One double crochet made. Work a double crochet (repeat Steps 1 through 3) in each remaining chain.

To work additional rows, make 3 chains and turn work counterclockwise. Beginning in 2nd stitch (**Fig 53**—3 chains count as first double crochet), work a double crochet (as before) in each stitch across (remember to insert hook under 2 top loops of stitch). At end of row, work last double crochet in the top chain of chain-3 (**Fig 54**).

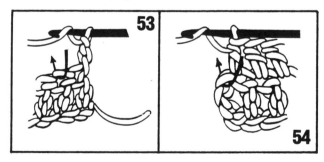

HALF DOUBLE CROCHET (hdc)

This stitch eliminates one step of double crochet—hence its name. It is taller than single crochet, but shorter than double crochet. Begin by making a chain to desired length.

Step 1: Bring yarn over hook; insert hook in top loop of 3rd chain from hook, hook yarn and draw through (3 loops now on hook).

Step 2: Hook yarn and draw through all 3 loops on hook (**Fig 55**).

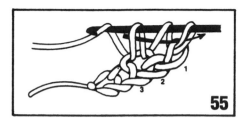

One half double crochet made. Work a half double crochet (repeat Steps 1 and 2) in each remaining chain.

To work additional rows, make 2 chains and turn work counterclockwise. Beginning in 2nd stitch (2 chains count as first half double crochet), work a half double crochet (as before) in each stitch across. At end of row, work last half double crochet in the top chain of chain-2.

TRIPLE CROCHET (tr)

Triple crochet is a tall stitch that works up quickly. First, make a chain to desired length.

Step 1: Bring yarn twice over the hook, insert hook in 5th chain from hook (**Fig 56**); hook yarn and draw through (**Fig 57**).

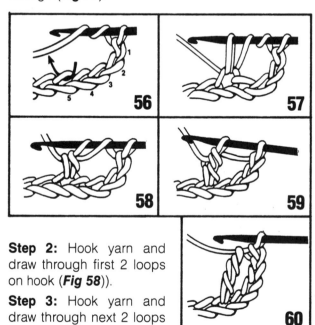

Step 2: Hook yarn and draw through first 2 loops on hook (**Fig 58**)).

Step 3: Hook yarn and draw through next 2 loops on hook (**Fig 59**).

Step 4: Hook yarn and draw through remaining 2 loops on hook (**Fig 60**).

One triple crochet made. Work a triple crochet (repeat Steps 1 through 4) in each remaining chain.

To work additional rows, make 4 chains and turn work counterclockwise. Beginning in 2nd stitch (4 chains count as first triple crochet), work a double crochet (as before) in each stitch across. At end of row, work last triple crochet in the top chain of chain-4.

SLIP STITCH (sl st)

This is the shortest of all crochet stitches, and usually is used to join work, or to move yarn across a group of stitches without adding height. To practice, make a chain to desired length; then work one row of double crochets.

Step 1: Insert hook in first st; hook yarn and draw through both stitch and loop on hook in one motion (**Fig 61**).

One slip stitch made. Work a slip stitch (repeat Step 1) in each stitch across.

INCREASING AND DECREASING

Shaping is usually accomplished either by increasing, which adds stitches to make the crocheted piece wider; or decreasing, which subtracts stitches to make the piece narrower.

Increasing: To increase one stitch—in single, half double, double or triple crochet, simply work two stitches in one stitch.

Decreasing: A simple method of decreasing is to skip a stitch, but this is usually undesirable, as it will leave a hole in your work. The preferred way is to work two stitches into one stitch. Practice each technique on a sample swatch of the stitch used in the decrease method.

Decreasing in Single Crochet: Draw up a loop in each of the next 2 stitches (3 loops now on hook), hook yarn and draw through all 3 loops on hook (**Fig 62**). Single crochet decrease made (**Fig 63**).

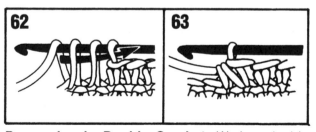

Decreasing in Double Crochet: Work a double crochet in the first stitch until 2 loops remain on hook (**Fig 64**). Keeping these 2 loops on hook, work another double crochet in the next (2nd) stitch until 3 loops remain on hook, hook yarn and draw through all 3 loops on hook (**Fig 65**). Double crochet decrease made (**Fig 66**).

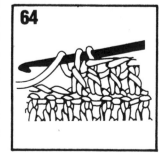

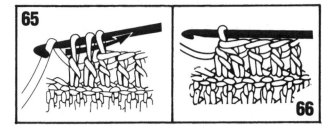

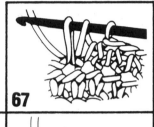

Decreasing in Half Double Crochet: Work a half double crochet in the first stitch until 3 loops remain on hook (*Fig 67*). Keeping these 3 loops on hook, draw up a loop in the next (2nd) stitch (4 loops now on hook), hook yarn and draw through all 4 loops on hook (*Fig 68*). Half double crochet decrease made (*Fig 69*).

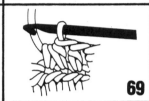

Decreasing in Triple Crochet: Work a triple crochet in the first stitch until 2 loops remain on hook (*Fig 70*). Keeping these 2 loops on hook, work another triple crochet in the next (2nd) stitch until 3 loops remain on hook, hook yarn and draw through all 3 loops on hook (*Fig 71*). Triple crochet decrease made (*Fig 72*).

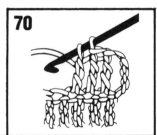

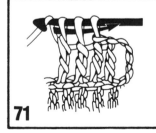
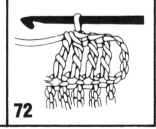

JOINING NEW YARN

Never tie or leave knots! In crochet, yarn ends can be easily worked in and hidden because of the density of the stitches. Always leave at least 4″ ends when finishing off yarn just used and joining new yarn. If a flaw or knot appears in the yarn while you are working from a ball or skein, cut out the imperfection and rejoin the yarn.

Whenever possible, join new yarn at the end of a row. To do this, work the last stitch with the old yarn until 2 loops remain on hook, then with new yarn complete the stitch (*Fig 73*).

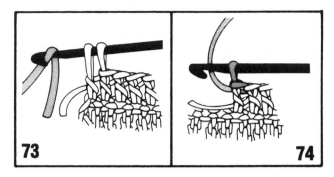

To join new yarn in the middle of a row, when about 12″ of the old yarn remains, work several more stitches with the old yarn, working the stitches over the end of new yarn. Then change yarns in stitch as previously explained (*Fig 74*). Continuing with new yarn, work the following stitches over the old yarn end.

GAUGE

This is the most important aspect of crochet—if you don't work to gauge, your crocheted projects will never be the correct size, and you may not have enough yarn to finish your project.

Gauge means the number of stitches per inch, and rows per inch, that result from a specified yarn worked with a specified size hook. But since everyone crochets differently—some loosely some tightly, some in between—the measurements of individual work can vary greatly when using the same size hook and yarn. It is your responsibility to make sure you achieve the gauge specified in the pattern.

Hook sizes given in instructions are merely guides and should never be used without making a 4″ square sample swatch to check gauge. Do not hesitate to change to a larger or smaller size hook if necessary to achieve gauge. If you get more stitches per inch than specified, try again with a larger size hook. If you get fewer stitches per inch than specified, try again with a smaller size hook. Keep trying until you find the size hook that will give you the specified gauge.

If you have the correct number of stitches per inch, but cannot achieve the row gauge, adjust the height of your stitches. This means that after inserting the hook to begin a new stitch, draw up a little more yarn if your stitches are not tall enough—this makes the first loop slightly higher; or draw up less yarn if your stitches are too tall. Practice will help you achieve the correct height.

FRINGE

BASIC INSTRUCTIONS

Cut a piece of cardboard about 6″ wide and half as long as specified in instructions for strands plus ½″ for trimming allowance. Wind yarn loosely and evenly lengthwise around cardboard. When card is filled, cut yarn across one end. Do this several times, then begin fringing; you can wind additional strands as you need them.

SINGLE KNOT FRINGE

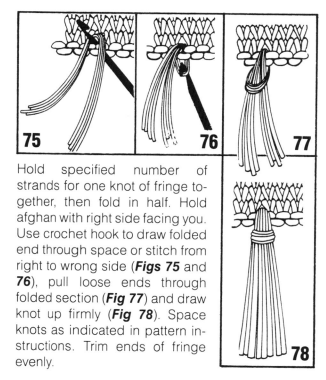

Hold specified number of strands for one knot of fringe together, then fold in half. Hold afghan with right side facing you. Use crochet hook to draw folded end through space or stitch from right to wrong side (**Figs 75** and **76**), pull loose ends through folded section (**Fig 77**) and draw knot up firmly (**Fig 78**). Space knots as indicated in pattern instructions. Trim ends of fringe evenly.

DOUBLE KNOT FRINGE

Begin by working Single Knot Fringe completely across one end of afghan. With right side facing you and working from left to right, take half the strands of one knot and half the strands in the knot next to it, and knot them together (**Fig 79**).

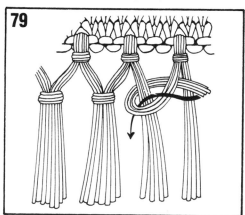

TRIPLE KNOT FRINGE

First work Double Knot Fringe. Then working again on right side from left to right, tie third row of knots as in **Fig 80**.

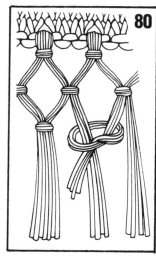

BASIC GRANNY SQUARE

This pattern lets you practice the basic techniques of granny squares, but when making a specific project in this book or any other source, follow the *exact* instructions given, as there are slight differences in working methods of different motifs.

Make a sl knot on hook with first color, leaving a 3″ end. Ch 4, join with a sl st to form a ring (**Fig 81**).

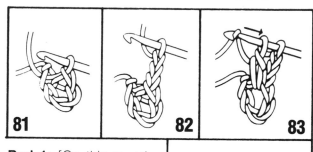

Rnd 1: [On this round, you will be working *into* the ring. As you do this, also work over the 3″ end left after making the sl knot; this keeps down the number of yarn ends to be run in after the square is completed.] Ch 3 (**Fig 82**), 2 dc in ring (**Fig 83** shows first dc being worked in ring);

(ch 2, 3 dc in ring) 3 times; ch 2, join in 3rd ch of beg ch-3 with a sl st (**Fig 84**). [The side of the work now facing you is called the *right side* of the work.] Finish off first color.

Rnd 2: Make a sl knot on hook with 2nd color; with right side of work facing you, join 2nd color with a sl st in any ch-2 sp (these are corner sps); ch 3, 2 dc in same sp (**Fig 85** shows first dc being worked in sp); ch 2, 3 dc again in same sp; * in next ch-2 sp, work (3 dc, ch 2, 3 dc); rep from * twice, join with a sl st in 3rd ch of beg ch-3. Finish off 2nd color. Look at your work; you should now have a perfect square.

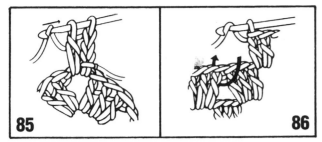

Rnd 3: With right side of work facing you, join 3rd color as before in any ch-2 corner sp; (ch 3, 2 dc, ch 2, 3 dc) all in same sp; between next two 3-dc groups (**Fig 86**), work 3 dc for side; * (3 dc, ch 2, 3 dc) all in next ch-2 sp for corner; 3 dc between next two 3-dc groups for side; rep from * twice, join with a sl st in 3rd ch of beg ch-3. Finish off 3rd color.

Rnd 4: With right side of work facing you, join 4th color as before in any ch-2 corner sp; (ch 3, 2 dc, ch 2, 3 dc) all in same sp; * (3 dc between next two 3-dc groups) twice for side; (3 dc, ch 2, 3 dc) all in next ch-2 sp for corner; rep from * twice; (3 dc between next two 3-dc groups) twice for side; join with a sl st in 3rd ch of beg ch-3. Finish off 4th color. Weave in all loose yarn ends; trim them off.

NOTES

1. You now have a 4-rnd square; work any additional desired rnds as for Rnd 4, working one more side group of 3 dcs on every additional rnd.

2. Unless a pattern specifies that you must *turn* your work before each new rnd, always work with the right side facing you.

3. When a pattern calls for working 2 or more rnds of the same color in succession, work to end of rnd, join, but do not finish off. Sl st in tops of each of next 2 dcs and into corner sp; work next rnd as specified.

4. When making grannys, you'll have lots of yarn ends to weave in (do this securely). Make it a practice to weave these in as you finish each square, unless the pattern says not to.

JOINING

When joining granny squares or other pieces of crochet, we often tell you to sew through back loops only. Do this with an overcast stitch, working through the loops as shown in **Fig 87**. Take care not to pull the sewing stitches too tightly.

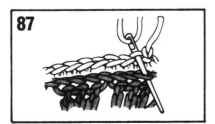

EDGINGS

Single Crochet Edging: Upon completion of a project, it is sometimes necessary to finish an edge. The instructions will say to "work a row of single crochet, taking care to keep work flat." This means to adjust your stitches as you work. You may need to skip a row or stitch here or there to keep the edging from rippling; or add a stitch to keep the work from pulling in. When working around a corner, it is usually necessary to work 3 stitches in the center corner stitch to keep the corner flat and square.

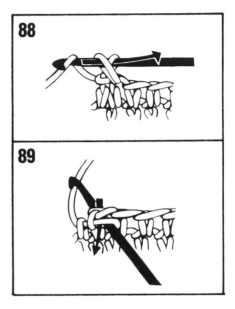

Reverse Single Crochet Edging: This edging produces a lovely corded effect and is usually worked after a row of single crochet. It is worked on the right side **from left to right** (the opposite direction for working single crochet). Work one reverse single crochet in each stitch across (see **Figs 88 and 89**).

LAZY DAISY STITCH EMBROIDERY

Here is how the stitch is worked to create charming small flowers (**Fig 90**). You can have 4, 5 or more petals, as you desire.

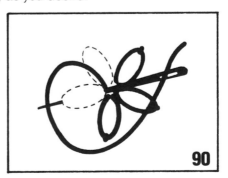

SYMBOLS

* An asterisk is used to mark the beginning of a portion of instructions which will be worked more than once; thus, "rep from * twice" means after working the instructions once, repeat the instructions following the asterisk twice more (3 times in all).

† The dagger identifies a portion of instructions that will be repeated again later in the pattern.

: The number after a colon at the end of a row indicates the number of stitches you should have when the row has been completed.

( ) Parentheses are used to enclose instructions which should be worked the exact number of times specified immediately following the parentheses, such as (K1, P1) twice. They are also used to set off and clarify a group of sts that are to be worked all into the same sp or st, such as (2 dc, ch 1, 2 dc) in corner sp.

[ ] Brackets and ( ) parentheses are used to provide additional information to clarify instructions.

ABBREVIATIONS

KNIT ABBREVIATIONS

BO	bind off
CO	cast on
dpn	double pointed needle
K	knit
P	purl
PSSO	pass slipped stitch over
stock st	stockinette stitch (knit 1 row, purl 1 row)

CROCHET ABBREVIATIONS

ch(s)	chain(s)
dc	double crochet(s)
hdc	half double crochet(s)
sc	single crochet(s)
sl st(s)	slip stitch(es)
Tch	turning chain
tr	triple crochet(s)

KNIT AND CROCHET ABBREVIATIONS

beg	begin(ning)	prev	previous	sl	slip
dec	decrease (-ing)	rem	remain(ing)	sp(s)	space(s)
Fig	figure	rep	repeat(ing)	st(s)	stitch(es)
inc	increase (-ing)	rnd(s)	round(s)	tog	together
patt	pattern	sk	skip	YO	yarn over

WORK EVEN   This term in instructions means to continue working in the pattern as established, without increasing or decreasing.

GRANNY AFGHANS
TO CROCHET

Probably the most popular afghan pattern of all time is the humble granny square. This is simply a square, worked in double or triple crochet, originally in left-over yarn colors combined with black.

But how far this humble square has come over the years! Talented crocheters have created squares with floral centers, with limitless color patterns, even squares that when sewn together make pictures.

Today crocheters use the term "granny square" rather loosely; it has come to mean any crocheted individual motif (whether square, octaganol or round).

Grannies are nicely portable; they are small, and can travel with you to the beauty shop, the doctor's waiting room or even (for shame!) to a party.

CLASSIC GRANNY

This is the classic granny with a twist: we've used ombre shades instead of solids for the centers of the squares. The first three rounds of each square are worked in an ombre, the fourth round in black. The look is bright and cheerful.

SIZE

48″ × 60″

MATERIALS

Worsted weight yarn, COATS & CLARK RED HEART®:
  - 10½ oz Ombre Roses
  - 7 oz Ombre Oranges
  - 10½ oz Ombre Greens
  - 14 oz Ombre Blues
  - 7 oz Black

Size I aluminum crochet hook (or size required for gauge)

GAUGE

1 square = 6″

NOTE

Make 20 Rose squares, 28 Blue, 20 Green, 12 Orange.

INSTRUCTIONS

With Ombre, ch 4; join with a sl st to form a ring.

Rnd 1: Ch 3 (counts as 1 dc), 2 dc in ring; * ch 3, 3 dc in ring; rep from * twice more, ch 3; join with a sl st to top of ch-3; slip st to ch-3 space.

Rnd 2: Ch 3, 2 dc in same space; * ch 2, in next space work (3 dc, ch 3, 3 dc); rep from * twice more, ch 2, 3 dc in same space as first ch-3, ch 3, join with sl st to top of ch-3; slip st to ch-3 space.

Rnd 3: Ch 3, 2 dc in same space; * ch 2, 3 dc in next space, ch 2; in corner space work (3 dc, ch 3, 3 dc); rep from *, ending ch 2, 3 dc in same space as first ch-3, ch 3, join with a sl st to top of ch-3. Fasten off.

Rnd 4: Join Black in any ch-3 sp; rep Rnd 3, having two groups of 3-dc between corners; fasten off.

Weave in all ombre yarn ends, but leave the black yarn ends for later.

JOINING

Squares are joined into 10 rows of 8 squares each. To join, hold two squares with right sides facing; sl st squares together loosely with black, inserting the hook into the back loops only of each square.

Join each *row* of squares first; tie a number on each finished row so that you don't get them mixed up later when joining row to row. Join squares in each row as follows (from left to right):

Row 1: 8 Rose.

Row 2: 8 Blue.

Row 3: 1 Blue, 6 Green, 1 Blue.

Row 4: 1 Blue, 1 Green, 4 Gold, 1 Green, 1 Blue.

Row 5: 1 Blue, 1 Green, 1 Gold, 2 Rose, 1 Gold, 1 Green, 1 Blue.

Row 6: Same as Row 5.

Row 7: Same as Row 4.

Row 8: Same as Row 3.

Row 9: Same as Row 2.

Row 10: Same as Row 1.

Now join the strips, slip stitching each strip to the one below, again with right sides facing and working into *back* loop of each stitch; carefully match stitches as you work, and work a ch-1 between each square (this keeps work flat). Weave in all loose black ends, running the ends into the seam of the next square, rather than back into the square itself.

EDGING

Join Black with a sl st into any outer corner ch-3 sp; work as for Rnd. 3 of square; work one more rnd in Black; finish off, weave in ends.

SUNFLOWER GRANNY

Popcorn stitches give a raised dimension to these bright squares. The afghan will bring sun to a cold wintery day.

SIZE

50" × 68"

MATERIALS

DAWN SAYELLE* knitting worsted weight yarn:
    28 oz Copper #359
    12 oz Orange #347
    12 oz Chocolate Brown #306A
    10 oz Shaded Beiges #379
Size I aluminum crochet hook (or size required for gauge)

GAUGE

One square = 9"

INSTRUCTIONS

SQUARE (make 35)

With Orange, ch 6, join with a sl st to form a ring.

Rnd 1: Work beg PC (popcorn) in ring as follows: Ch 3, work 3 dc in ring; drop lp from hook, insert hook in top of beg ch-3; hook dropped lp and pull through st (**Fig 1**) = beg PC made * Ch 3, work PC in ring as follows: Work 4 dc in ring; drop lp from hook, insert hook in first dc of 4-dc group just made; hook dropped lp and pull through st = PC made. Rep from * twice more; ch 3, join with a sl st in top of ch-3 of beg PC. Do not finish off.

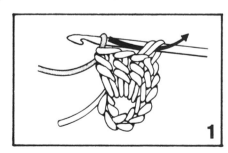

Rnd 2: Continuing with Orange, sl st into next ch-3 sp; work (beg PC, ch 3, PC) in same sp; * ch 3, work (PC, ch 3, PC) in next ch-3 sp; rep from * twice more; ch 3, join with a sl st in top of ch-3 of beg PC. Finish off Orange.

Rnd 3: With Shaded Beiges, join with a sl st in any ch-3 sp between 2 PCs worked into the SAME sp; ch 3, 2 dc in same sp; work (3 dc, ch 3, 3 dc) in next ch-3 sp for corner; * work 3 dc in next ch-3 sp (between 2 PCs worked into the same sp), work (3 dc, ch 3, 3 dc) in next ch-3 sp for corner; rep from * twice more; join with a sl st in top of beg ch-3. Do not finish off.

Rnd 4: Continuing with Shaded Beiges, sl st in each of next 2 dc, then sl st into sp between pair of 3-dc groups, ch 3, 2 dc in same sp; work (3 dc, ch 3, 3 dc) in next ch-3 sp at corner; * work 3 dc between each pair of 3-dc groups along side, work (3 dc, ch 3, 3 dc) in next ch-3 sp at corner; rep from * twice more; work 3 dc between last pair of 3-dc groups, join with a sl st in top of beg ch-3. Finish off Shaded Beiges.

Rnd 5: With Copper, join with a sl st in any corner ch-3 sp; ch 3, work (2 dc, ch 3, 3 dc) in same sp; * work 3 dc between each pair of 3-dc groups along side, work (3 dc, ch 3, 3 dc) in next ch-3 sp at corner; rep from * twice more; work 3 dc between each pair of 3-dc groups along last side, join with a sl st in top of beg ch-3. Do not finish off.

Rnd 6: Continuing with Copper sl st in each of next 2 dc, then sl st into ch-3 corner sp; now work rnd in same manner as Rnd 5. Do not finish off.

Rnd 7: Rep Rnd 6. Finish off Copper.

Rnd 8: With Chocolate Brown, rep Rnd 5. Finish off; weave in all ends.

FINISHING

Afghan is 5 squares wide by 7 squares long. Join squares tog, with right sides facing, working sc through back lp only of each stitch.

BORDER

With right side facing you, join Chocolate Brown with a sl st in any ch-3 corner sp of afghan. Working in same manner as Rnd 5 of Square, work one rnd in each of the following colors: Chocolate Brown, Orange, Shaded Beiges and Copper. When all 4 rnds of border have been completed, finish off and weave in all loose yarn ends.

ICE CRYSTALS

Pure white crystals against a shimmering blue background makes this an especially striking afghan. Two different motifs are used.

SIZE

47″ × 72″ before fringing

MATERIALS

Mohair type worsted weight yarn, CARON
   DAZZLEAIRE:
      30 oz Sky Blue
      12 oz White
Size G aluminum crochet hook (or size required for
   gauge)

GAUGE

Each motif = 6″ from side edge to side edge;
                  6½″ from point to point.

INSTRUCTIONS

SOLID MOTIFS (make 68)

Rnd 1: With Sky Blue, ch 6; in 6th ch from hook work (dc, ch 3) 5 times; join with a sl st to 3rd ch of starting ch; you should have 6 dc and 6 ch-3 spaces.

Rnd 2: Sl st into first sp, ch 3 (counts as first dc), work 2 dc in same sp, ch 3; (work 3 dc in next sp, ch 3) 5 times, join with a sl st to 3rd ch of starting ch.

Rnd 3: Ch 4 (counts as first tr); 1 tr in each of next 2 dc; * work (2 tr, ch 3, 2 tr) all in next ch-3 sp; 1 tr in each of next 3 dc; rep from * 4 times more, end with (2 tr, ch 3, 2 tr) all in last ch-3 sp; join with sl st in 4th ch of starting chain; you should have 7 dc on each of 6 sides with ch-3 sp between.

Rnd 4: Ch 4 (counts as first dc and ch-1 sp); (skip 1 st, dc in next tr, ch 1) twice; * work (1 dc, ch 3, 1 dc) all in ch-3 sp for corner; ch 1, dc in next tr; (ch 1, skip 1 st, dc in next tr) 3 times, ch 1; rep from * 4 times more, end with (1 dc, ch 3, 1 dc) all in last ch-3 sp; ch 1, dc in next tr, ch 1, skip last tr, join with sl st in 3rd ch of starting chain; you should have 6 dc and 5 ch-1 sps on each side between ch-3 corner sps; fasten off. Weave in yarn ends.

ICE CRYSTAL MOTIFS (make 36)

Rnd 1: With White ch 6; in 6th ch from hook work (dc, ch 3) 5 times; join with sl st in 3rd ch of starting ch; you should have 6 dc and 6 ch-3 sps.

Rnd 2: Sl st into first sp, ch 1; * work 1 hdc in ch-3 sp, 1 dc in same sp; ch 6, sl st in 3rd ch from hook and in each of rem 3 ch for long picot; 1 dc in same sp, 1 hdc in same sp; ch 5; sl st in 3rd ch from hook for short picot, ch 2; rep from * in each of rem 5 sps around, join with sl st in first hdc; you should have 6 long picots and 6 short picots; fasten off white.

Rnd 3: Join blue with sl st in top of any short picot, ch 1; * sc in top of short picot, at base of next long picot work 1 tr in first hdc, 2 tr in dc, ch 1, sl st in top of long picot, ch 1; on other side of same picot work 2 tr in dc, 1 tr in hdc; rep from * 5 times more, join with sl st in first sc.

Rnd 4: Sl st into first tr, ch 4 (counts as first dc and ch-1 sp); skip 1 st, dc in next tr, ch 1; * work (1 dc, ch 3, 1 dc) all in sl st at top of long picot for corner; ch 1, dc in next tr, (ch 1, skip 1 st, dc in next tr) 3 times, ch 1; rep from * 4 times more, end with (1 dc, ch 3, 1 dc) all in sl st at top of last long picot, ch 1, dc in next tr, ch 1, skip 1 st, dc in next tr, ch 1, join with sl st in 3rd ch of starting chain; you should have 6 dc and 5 ch-1 sps on each of 6 sides between ch-3 corner sps; fasten off. Weave in yarn ends.

JOINING

Arrange motifs as shown in Arrangement Chart. Working from the right side of each motif with care to keep seams flat, use a blunt needle and blue to sew motifs tog with an overhand st **through the back lps only** of corresponding sts.

EDGING

From right side, join blue with a sl st in any ch-3

ARRANGEMENT CHART

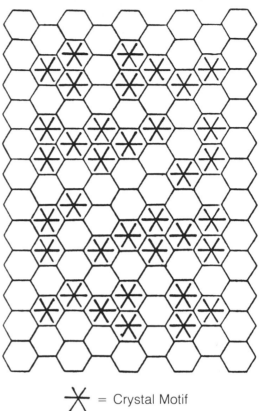

✳ = Crystal Motif

corner sp on outside edge; ch 1, work 3 sc in each corner sp, 1 sc in each dc and in each ch-1 sp along edge of motif to last dc before joining seam; draw up a lp in each corner sp on both sides of seam, YO and through all 3 lps on hook for dec; continue all around outside edge in same way, join with sl st in first sc and fasten off.

FRINGE

With white, cut two lengths fringe: 14" strands for longer panels, 20 strands for shorter panels. Following Single Knot Fringe instructions on page 16, use 4 strands doubled for each knot. Tie one knot in each of 7 spaces across lower edge of each motif on both short ends.

DAISY FIELD BABY GRANNY

Bright white and shaded yellows create the soft flowers in this pretty afghan for baby. After the squares are joined, you embroider Lazy Daisy stitches at each intersection of four squares.

SIZE

28" × 32"

MATERIALS

Mohair type worsted weight yarn, CARON DAZZELEAIRE:
    8 oz White
    12 oz Shaded Yellows
Size H aluminum crochet hook (or size required for gauge)
Size 16 tapestry needle for joining and embroidery.

GAUGE

One square = 3¾"

INSTRUCTIONS

GRANNY SQUARE (make 56)

With Shaded Yellows, ch 4, join with a sl st to form a ring.

Rnd 1: Work 8 sc in ring, join.

Rnd 2: Ch 3; in same sc, (YO, draw up a lp) twice, YO and draw through all 5 lps on hook: cluster made; * ch 3; in next sc, (YO, draw up a lp) 3 times, YO and draw through all 7 lps on hook: cluster made; rep from * around, ch 3, join with a sl st to top of beg ch-3; finish off Shaded Yellows.

Rnd 3: Join White in any ch-3 sp; for corner, ch 3, 4 dc in same sp; * 4 dc in next ch-3 sp, 5 dc in next ch-3 sp for corner; rep from * twice more, 4 dc in next ch-3 sp, join with a sl st to top of beg ch-3; finish off White.

Rnd 4: Join Shaded Yellows in top of center dc of any 5-dc corner group; ch 3, 4 dc in same st; * dc in each st to center dc of next 5-dc corner group; 5 dc in center st; rep from * twice more, dc in each st to beg, join with a sl st to top of beg ch-3; finish off.

JOINING

To join, hold two squares with right sides together and with Shaded Yellows, sew through back loops only, carefully matching stitches. Join squares in 7 rows of 8 squares each.

EDGING

Hold afghan with right side facing you.

Rnd 1: Join White with a sl st in center st of 5-dc group at any outer corner of afghan; ch 3, 4 dc in same st; dc in each dc and in each joining between squares to center st of 5-dc group at next corner, work 5 dc in center st; continue in this manner around to beg, join with a sl st to top of beg ch-3; finish off White.

Rnd 2: Join Shaded Yellows with a sl st in center dc of 5-dc group at any corner; 3 sc in this st, sc in each dc to center st of 5-dc group at next corner; continue in this manner around to beg, join with a sl st to beg sc.

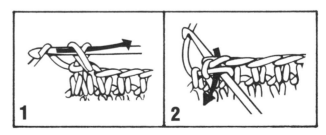

Rnd 3: Work in reverse single crochet. This stitch is worked on the right side **from left to right** (**Figs 1 and 2**). This is the opposite direction for working the regular single crochet stitch. Work one reverse single crochet in each stitch across; finish off and weave in ends.

EMBROIDERY

With Shaded Yellows, work a four-petal Lazy Daisy embroidery stitch (see page 17) wherever four corners join.

NASTURTIUMS
GRANNY LAPGHAN AND PILLOW

Our Lapghan is the perfect size to warm your knees and legs while you sit in a chair or watch TV. To make you even more comfy, we've included a matching pillow to tuck behind your back. The set would make a wonderful gift for a nursing home patient, or for someone confined to a wheelchair.

SIZE

40″ × 40″

MATERIALS

Worsted weight yarn, COATS & CLARK RED
  HEART®:
    3½ oz each of:
      Vermillion   Orange
      Jockey Red   Gold
      Scarlet   Yellow
      Maize   Burnt Orange
      Tangerine
    14 oz White
Size H aluminum crochet hook (or size required for
  gauge)
16″ Pillow Form

GAUGE

1 square = 5¼″

AFGHAN INSTRUCTIONS

Make 6 squares of Vermillion, 5 squares each of Jockey Red and Scarlet; 4 squares each of Burnt Orange and Gold; 3 squares each of Tangerine, Orange, Maize and Yellow.

GRANNY SQUARE

Using any color but white, ch 4, sl st to form a ring.

Rnd 1: Ch 3, (counts as 1 dc), 2 dc in ring; * ch 2, 3 dc in ring; rep from * twice more, ch 2; join with a sl st to top of ch-3; slip st to ch-2 space.

Rnd 2: Ch 3, 2 dc in same space; * ch 1, in next space, work (3 dc, ch 2, 3 dc); Repeat from * twice more, ch 1, 3 dc in same space as first ch-2, ch 2; join with sl st to top of ch-3; slip st to ch-2 space.

Rnd 3: Ch 3, 2 dc in same space; * ch 1, 3 dc in next space, ch 1. In corner space work (3 dc, ch 2, 3 dc); rep from * ending ch 1, 3 dc in same space as first ch-3, ch 1, join with sl st to top of ch-3; fasten off.

Rnd 4: Join White in any ch-2 space. Repeat Rnd 3 having 2 groups of 3 dc between corners. Fasten off white, weave in all yarn ends.

JOINING

Squares are joined into 6 rows of 6 squares each. To join, hold two squares with right sides facing; sl st squares together loosely with white, inserting the hook into the back loops only of each square.

Join each *row* of squares first; tie a number on each finished row so that you don't get them mixed up later when joining row to row. Join squares in each row as follows (from left to right):

Row 1: Vermillion, Scarlet, Burnt Orange, Tangerine, Orange, Orange.

Row 2: Jockey Red, Vermillion, Scarlet, Burnt Orange, Tangerine, Orange.

Row 3: Gold, Jockey Red, Vermillion, Scarlet, Burnt Orange, Tangerine.

Row 4: Maize, Gold, Jockey Red, Vermillion, Scarlet, Burnt Orange.

Row 5: Yellow, Maize, Gold, Jockey Red, Vermillion, Scarlet.

Row 6: Yellow, Yellow, Maize, Gold, Jockey Red, Vermillion.

Now join the strips, slip stitching each strip to the one below, again with right sides facing and working into back loop of each stitch; carefully match stitches as you work, and work a ch-1 between each square (this keeps work flat). Weave in all loose ends.

EDGING

Join white with a sl st in any ch-2 corner sp; work 3 rnds in Granny Square pattern, finish off.

PILLOW

Work two squares in each color. For each pillow side, join squares as for afghan in 3 rows of 3 squares, arranging colors as you choose.

To finish pillow, place the two pillow squares with wrong sides together, and working through both layers, join white with a sl st in any ch-2 corner sp; work around 3 sides in Granny Square pattern, working (3dc, ch 2, 3 dc) in each corner sp; insert pillow form, continue to close fourth side of pillow. Work one more round in white, finish off. Weave in ends.

FLOWER GARDEN

This lovely pattern is made in easy motifs with a pretty combination of colors to create a charming floral design.

SIZE

46" × 65"

MATERIALS

Worsted weight yarn:
    13 oz Lemon Yellow
    10 oz Peach
     8 oz Raspberry
     5 oz Spring Green
    13 oz White
Size I aluminum crochet hook (or size required for gauge)

GAUGE

One square = 9½"

INSTRUCTIONS

SQUARE *(make 24)*

With yellow, ch 5, join with a sl st to form a ring.

Rnd 1 (right side): Ch 4 (counts as first trc of rnd), trc in ring; * ch 2, 2 trc in ring; rep from * 6 times more, ch 2, join with a sl st in top of beg ch-4: eight 2-trc groups + 8 ch-2 sps. Finish off yellow.

Rnd 2: With right side facing you, join peach with a sl st in first trc of any 2-trc group, ch 3 (counts as first dc of rnd), 2 dc in next trc; * ch 2, sk next ch-2 sp, dc in next trc, 2 dc in next trc; rep from * 6 times more, ch 2, sk last ch-2 sp, join with a sl st in top of beg ch-3: eight 3-dc groups + 8 ch-2 sps. DO NOT finish off.

Rnd 3: Continuing with peach, ch 3, do not turn; work 3 dc in next dc, dc in next dc; * ch 2, sk next ch-2 sp, dc in next dc, 3 dc in next dc, dc in next dc; rep from * 6 times more, ch 2, sk last ch-2 sp, join with a sl st in top of beg ch-3: eight 5-dc groups + 8 ch-2 sps. Finish off peach.

Rnd 4: With right side facing you, join raspberry with a sl st in first dc of any 5-dc group, ch 3, dc in next dc, 3 dc in next dc, dc in each of next 2 dc; * ch 2, sk next ch-2 sp, dc in each of next 2 dc, 3 dc in next dc, dc in each of next 2 dc; rep from * 6 times more, ch 2, sk last ch-2 sp, join with a sl st in top of beg ch-3: eight 7-dc groups + 8 ch-2 sps. Finish off raspberry.

Rnd 5: With right side facing you, join green with a sl st in first dc of any 7-dc group, ch 3, dc in each of next 3 dc; * † 2 dc in next dc, trc in each of next 2 dc; ch 2 (for corner sp), sk next ch-2 sp, trc in each of next 2 dc; 2 dc in next dc, dc in each of next 4 dc †; ch 2 (for sp at center of side), sk next ch-2 sp, dc in each of next 4 dc; rep from * twice more, then rep from † to † once, ch 2, sk last ch-2 sp, join with a sl st in top of beg ch-3: four ch-2 corner sps (between trcs). Finish off green.

Rnd 6: With right side facing you, join white with a sl st in ch-2 sp between 2 trc at any corner, ch 3, work (dc, ch 3, 2 dc) in same sp; * dc in next st, hdc in each of next 3 sts, dec over next 2 sts as follows: Draw up a lp in each of next 2 sts (3 lps now on hook), YO hook and draw through all 3 lps on hook (dec made); sc in each of next 2 sts, ch 2, sk next ch-2 sp, sc in each of next 2 sts, dec over next 2 sts (as before); hdc in each of next 3 sts, dc in next st, work (2 dc, ch 3, 2 dc) in next ch-2 sp at corner; rep from * around, ending last rep without working corner, join with a sl st in top of beg ch-3. DO NOT finish off.

Rnd 7: Continuing with white, ch 3, do not turn; dc in next st, * work (2 dc, ch 3, 2 dc) in next ch-3 sp at corner, dc in each of next 9 sts; ch 2, sk next ch-2 sp, dc in each of next 9 sts; rep from * around, ending last rep by working dc in each of next 7 dc (instead of dc in each of next 9 sts), join with a sl st in top of beg ch-3. DO NOT finish off.

Rnd 8: Continuing with white, ch 3, do not turn; dc in each of next 3 sts, * work (2 dc, ch 3, 2 dc) in ch-3 sp at corner, dc in each of next 11 dc; ch 2, sk next ch-2 sp, dc in each of next 11 dc; rep from * around, ending last rep by working dc in each of next 7 dc (instead of dc in each of next 11 dc), join with a sl st in top of beg ch-3. Finish off white.

Rnd 9: With right side facing you, join yellow with a sl st in ch-3 sp at any corner, ch 3, work (dc, ch 3, 2 dc) in same sp; * dc in each of next 13 dc, ch 2, sk next ch-2 sp, dc in each of next 13 dc, work (2 dc, ch 3, 2 dc) in ch-3 sp at next corner; rep from * around, ending last rep without working last corner, join with a sl st in top of beg ch-3. Finish off, leaving approx 30" sewing length.

ASSEMBLING

Afghan is 4 squares wide by 6 squares long. To join two squares, hold both squares with right sides tog, with sewing length positioned whenever possible at upper right-hand corner. Thread sewing length (or use a length of matching yarn) into tapestry or yarn needle; weave to center ch st at corner. Now sew with overcast st **in outer lps only** of corresponding sts across, ending in center ch st at next corner. Continue to join squares in this manner until all squares are joined into rows. Then join rows tog in same manner, being careful that each 4-corner junction is firmly joined.

EDGING

Rnd 1: With right side facing you, join yellow with a sl st in ch-3 sp at any outer corner of afghan, ch 3, work (dc, ch 3, 2 dc) in same sp; dc in each of next 15 dc, dc in next ch-2 sp, dc in each of next 15 dc, * work 2 dc in each of next 2 sps (sp on each side of joining), dc in each of next 15 dc, dc in next ch-2 sp, dc in each of next 15 dc; rep from * across side to next corner, work (2 dc, ch 3, 2 dc) in corner ch-3 sp. Work rem sides and corners in same manner, join with a sl st in top of beg ch-3. DO NOT finish off.

Rnd 2: Continuing with yellow, ch 3, do not turn; dc in next dc, * work (2 dc, ch 3, 2 dc) in next corner sp, work dc in each dc across side; rep from * around, join with a sl st in top of beg ch-3. DO NOT finish off.

Rnd 3: Continuing with yellow, ch 3, do not turn; dc in each of next 3 dc, * work (2 dc, ch 3, 2 dc) in next corner sp, work dc in each dc across side; rep from * around, join with a sl st in top of beg ch-3. Finish off yellow.

Rnd 4: With right side facing you, join peach with a sl st in any corner sp, ch 3, work (dc, ch 3, 2 dc) in same sp; * work dc in each dc across side, work (2 dc, ch 3, 2 dc) in next corner sp; rep from * around, ending last rep without working corner, join with a sl st in top of beg ch-3. DO NOT finish off.

Rnds 5 and 6: Continuing with peach, rep Rnds 2 and 3. At end of Rnd 6, finish off peach.

Rnd 7: With raspberry, rep Rnd 4. DO NOT finish off.

Rnd 8: Continuing with raspberry, rep Rnd 2. Finish off and weave in all ends. Lightly steam press on wrong side.

[Chapter continued on page 49]

SILENT STAR

MULTI-COLOR STRIPED DELIGHT / GOLDEN PLAID

EMERALD ISLE

OCEAN WAVES

PINK PERFECTION

ICE CRYSTALS / CLASSIC GRANNY / ROSE GARDEN

LILAC TIME / SUMMER SKIES

35

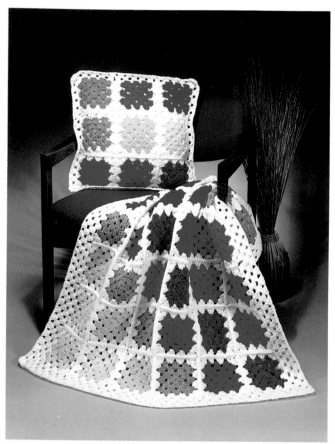

NASTURTIUM GRANNY LAPGHAN & PILLOW

FLOWER GARDEN

BLAZING SUNSET

LEMON LACE / SUNSHINE GRANNY

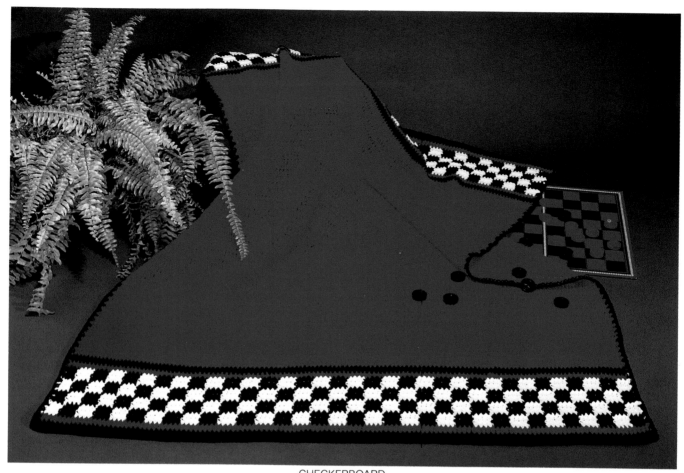

CHECKERBOARD

FREIGHT TRAIN

DAISY FIELD BABY GRANNY

DAFFODIL

PINK PETALS

FISHERMAN CABLES & LATTICE

39

PASTEL RAINBOW / LAVENDER LACE

SEDONA ROCKS / BRIGHT WAVES

GOLDEN SUNRISE / EASY GRANNY / EASY FEATHER & FAN / MOCK FISHERMAN

BRIGHT 'N BOLD GRANNY

SAMPLER STRIPES

DIAGONAL CHEVRONS

RIPPLING SHELLS / BEAUTIFUL BOBBLES

SUNFLOWER GRANNY

BROWN SHADED RIPPLE

SWEET SHELLS / SPRING GREEN

BLUE LACE / PRIMROSE CABLES / FEATHER & FAN

STRIPES ON PARADE / IN THE PINK

LAVENDER DAISIES / BLUE BOY

BLUE RHAPSODY / FUCHSIA BLOSSOMS

HEIRLOOM CHRISTENING BLANKET / GINGHAM & LACE

HORSESHOE CABLES

PASTEL CAROUSEL

QUICK LACE

YELLOW ROSE RIPPLE

LEMON-LIME STRIPE

CARAMELS & CREAM / FISHERMAN / DESERT SANDS

48

BRIGHT 'N BOLD GRANNY

Granny would sit bolt upright in her rocking chair if she could see this modern adaptation of the classic design. A center panel of brightly colored squares is surrounded by a geometric arrangement of black and white.

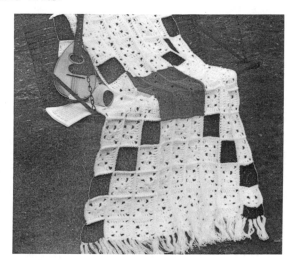

SIZE

45" × 65"

MATERIALS

COATS & CLARK RED HEART® 4-ply handknitting yarn, Art. E. 267:

52 oz White #1
12 oz Black #12

one skein each of:
Vibrant Orange #251
Burnt Orange #255
Ultra Pink #739

Size K aluminum crochet hook (or size required for gauge)

GAUGE

With 2 strands of yarn, each square measures 5"

INSTRUCTIONS

GRANNY SQUARE MOTIF (make 1 Pink; 4 Burnt Orange; 4 Vibrant Orange; 16 Black and 92 White)

With 2 strands held together, ch 4; join with a sl st to form a ring.

Rnd 1: Ch 4, 2 tr in ring, ch 3; (3 tr in ring, ch 3) 3 times; join to top of ch-4.

Rnd 2: Ch 4, tr in next 2 tr, * in next sp work (3 tr, ch 3, 3 tr); tr in next 3 tr. Repeat from * around, joining last tr to top of ch-4; fasten off.

JOINING

Motifs are crocheted together in vertical and horizontal rows with double strand of yarn. For joining the 15 center motifs, use colors indicated on Joining Chart. Use White for joining of all remaining motifs. Following chart for position of motifs, work all vertical rows first, then all horizontal rows as follows:

CHART

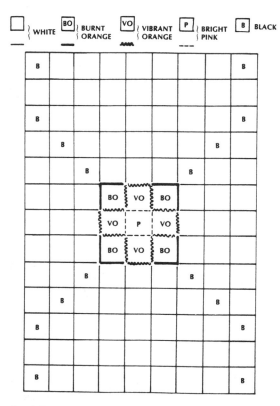

Vertical Rows: With wrong sides of motifs held together and picking up the *inside* loops only of sts to be joined, attach double strand to center ch of corner. Ch 1, sc through the 2 inside loops of each st to center st of next corner of same 2 motifs. Do not break off, but continue joining all motifs in same manner for length of afghan. Fasten off.

Horizontal Rows: Work as for Vertical rows, but make a ch 2 at each crossing of vertical rows and skip the 2 sc's underneath.

FRINGE

Following Single Knot Fringe instructions on page 16, cut strands of White each 16 inches long. Fold four strands in half for each knot. Space 6 knots evenly along each motif across each narrow edge.

ROSE GARDEN GRANNY

Take a nap under a beautiful rose garden! You'll have fun making as well as using this gorgeous afghan, featuring dimensional full-blown roses in the center of each motif.

SIZE

47" × 54"

MATERIALS

Mohair type worsted weight yarn, CARON DAZZLEAIRE:
   9 oz White #2601 Color A
   24 oz Azalea #2628 Color B
   15 oz Raspberry Punch #2686 Color C
Size I aluminum crochet hook (or size required for gauge)

GAUGE

1 square = 9"

INSTRUCTIONS

SQUARE (make 30)

Using Color A, ch 4; join with a slip stitch to form a ring.

Rnd 1: Ch 3, (2 dc, ch 2, 3 dc) in ring; * (3 dc, ch 2, 3 dc) in ring; rep from * twice more; ch 2, sl st to top of ch-3.

Rnd 2: Sl st into ch-2 space; ch 3, (2 dc, ch 2, 3 dc) in same space; * (3 dc, ch 2, 3 dc) in next ch-2 space; rep from * twice more; sl st into top of ch-3.

Rnd 3: Sl st into ch-2 space; ch 3, (2 dc, ch 2, 3 dc) in same space; * 3 dc between 3-dc corner groups; rep from * twice more; sl st into top of ch-3; Fasten off.

Rnd 4: Attach Color B in any ch-2 corner sp of previous rnd; (ch 3, dc, ch 2, 2 dc) all in same sp; * dc in next 3 dc, * dc between the 3-dc groups; rep from * to corner sp; (2 dc, ch 2, 2 dc) in ch-2 corner space; continue in this manner around, ending sl st into top of ch-3.

Rnd 5: Work in same manner as Rnd 4.

Rnd 6: Ch 1, 3 sc in corner sp; * sc in each dc to next ch-2 corner space; 3 sc in ch-2 space; work in this manner around, ending sl st into ch-1, ch 1.

Rnd 7: Sc in each sc around, working 3 sc in center sc of each corner; sl st into ch-1, ch 1.

Rnd 8: Repeat Row 7. Fasten off.

Rnd 9: Attach Color C to first sc beyond the 3-sc in any corner space; ch 1, sc in same space (short stitch); sc in sc in next row below (long stitch); * work 12 short and 11 long stitches to next corner. In corner space, work (2 long stitches, ch 2, 2 long stitches) into 2nd sc row below. Repeat from *, ending sl st in ch-1; fasten off. Weave in all yarn ends.

ROSES (make 30)

Using Color C, ch 4; join with a slip stitch to form a ring.

Rnd 1: * Ch 4, sc in ring; rep from * 5 more times; (6 loops).

Rnd 2: In each loop work petal of (1 sc, 1 hdc, 2 dc, 1 hdc, 1 sc); end with a sl st between 2 loops of previous row; (6 petals made).

Rnd 3: * Ch 4, sl st in the BACK of the sc between the next 2 petals; Rep from * 5 more times; (6 loops).

Rnd 4: In each loop work petal of (1 sc, 1 hdc, 3 dc, 1 hdc, 1 sc); sl st in 1st sc of first petal; sl st in stitch below. Fasten off. Weave in yarn ends.

Sew one rose into the center of each square; sew through flower and square centers, then sew two opposite petals to square; let remaining petals hang free.

FINISHING

To join squares into strips: Place squares together with RIGHT sides facing. With Color C, slip stitch squares together LOOSELY, inserting the hook into the **back** loops only of each square. Attach 5 squares across making a strip (6 strips altogether).

To join strips: Place strips together with RIGHT sides facing; with Color A, slip stitch squares together loosely, inserting the hook into the **back** loops only of each square. At the end of each square, ch 1, then slip stitch across next square. Repeat across all 5 squares.

BORDER

Attach Color C to a ch-2 space in a corner; * ch 4, sl st in base of ch-4, (picot made); 1 sc in next 4 sc; rep from * across to the joining of the first 2 squares. Work a picot in the ch-2 space of the 9th row of that square. Work 2 sc in seam, work a picot in the ch-2 space of the 9th row in the next square; 1 sc in next 4 sc; rep from * across entire row to the corner. Work a picot, ch 2, work a picot in the corner. Work 1 sc in next 4 sc, then a picot, following as before. Complete the 3 sides, ending with a picot, ch 2 in the beginning corner.

EASY GRANNY

This is a variation of the traditional granny afghan, which used leftover scraps of brightly colored yarns, bordered with black. In our version, we've used four bright ombre yarns with the black.

SIZE

43" × 63"

MATERIALS

Worsted weight yarn:
      6 oz Pink Ombre A
      6 oz Blue Ombre B
      6 oz Green Ombre C
      6 oz Orange Ombre D
      28 oz Black
Size I aluminum crochet hook (or size required for gauge)

GAUGE

One square = 10"

INSTRUCTIONS

SQUARE (make 6 with each ombre color, 24 squares in all)

With black, make a sl knot on hook, leaving a 3" end; ch 4, join with a sl st to form a ring.

NOTE

On first rnd, work over the 3" end to keep down the number of ends to be run in after the square is completed.

Rnd 1: Ch 3, 2 dc in ring; (ch 2, 3 dc in ring) 3 times; ch 2, join with a sl st in 3rd ch of beg ch-3. Finish off black. The side now facing you is right side.

Rnd 2: With ombre, make a sl knot on hook. With right side of Rnd 1 facing you, join ombre with a sl st in any ch-2 sp (these are corner sps); ch 3, 2 dc in same sp; ch 2, 3 dc again in same sp; * in next ch-2 sp, work (3 dc, ch 2, 3 dc); rep from * twice, join with a sl st in 3rd ch of beg ch-3; sl st across tops of next 2 dc and into ch-2 sp.

Rnd 3: Continuing with ombre, in same ch-2 sp, (ch 3, 2 dc in sp; ch 2, 3 dc in sp); between next two 3-dc groups work 3 dc for side; * (3 dc, ch 2, 3 dc) all in next ch-2 sp for corner; 3 dc between next two 3-dc groups for side; rep from * twice, join with a sl st in 3rd ch of beg ch-3; finish off ombre.

Rnd 4: With right side of work facing, join black as before in any ch-2 corner sp; (ch 3, 2 dc, ch 2, 3 dc) all in same sp; * (3 dc between next two 3-dc groups) twice for side; (3 dc, ch 2, 3 dc) all in next ch-2 sp for corner; rep from * twice; (3 dc between next two 3-dc groups) twice for side; join with a sl st in 3rd ch of beg ch-3; sl st across tops of next 2 dc and into ch-2 sp.

Rnd 5: Continuing with black, (ch 3, 2 dc, ch 2, 3 dc) all in same corner sp; * (3 dc between next two 3-dc groups) 3 times for side; (3 dc, ch 2, 3 dc) in next ch-2 sp for corner; rep from * twice; (3 dc between next two 3-dc groups) 3 times for side; join with a sl st in 3rd ch of beg ch-3; finish off black.

Rnd 6: Join ombre as before in any ch-2 corner sp; (ch 3, 2 dc, ch 2, 3 dc) all in same sp; * 3 dc between every 3-dc group for side; (3 dc, ch 2, 3 dc) in next ch-2 sp; rep from * twice; 3 dc between every 3-dc group for side; join with a sl st in 3rd ch of beg ch-3; sl st across tops of next 2 dc and into ch-2 sp.

Rnd 7: Continuing with ombre, (ch 3, 2 dc, ch 2, 3 dc) all in same sp; * 3 dc between every 3-dc group for side; (3 dc, ch 2, 3 dc) in next ch-2 sp; rep from * twice; 3 dc between every 3-dc group for side; join with a sl st in 3rd ch of beg ch-3; sl st across tops of next 2 dc and into ch-2 sp.

Rnd 8: Rep Rnd 7, but finish by joining with a sl st in 3rd ch of beg ch-3; finish off ombre.

Rnd 9: With black, rep Rnd 6.

Rnd 10: Continuing with black, rep Rnd 7, but finish by joining with a sl st in 3rd ch of beg ch-3; finish off black.

Weave in all loose ends.

GRANNY'S PICTURE AFGHANS

The following two afghans are called Picture Afghans; they are both made from Granny Squares. We've given you a delightful Freight Train to warm the heart of any child and an adaptation of an old quilt design, called Silent Star. We think you'll enjoy learning the special techniques to make these unusual afghans.

BASIC PICTURE AFGHAN INSTRUCTIONS

Both of our Picture Afghans are made of 2-rnd granny squares: one-color, two-color (*different color used for each rnd*), and diagonal two-color (*resembles a pair of joined triangles*). To make squares, use size G aluminum crochet hook—or size required for gauge (*one square = 2¼"*). Colors or combination of colors for squares are listed with the individual pattern instructions.

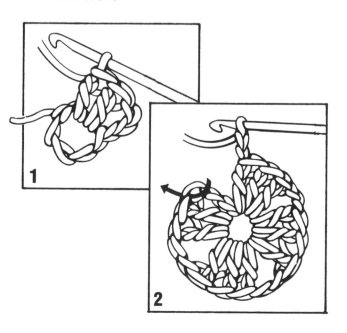

ONE-COLOR SQUARE

Ch 4, join with a sl st to form a ring.

Rnd 1 (wrong side): Ch 3, 2 dc in ring (**Fig 1**); * ch 2, 3 dc in ring; rep from * twice more; ch 2, join with a sl st in top of beg ch-3 (**Fig 2**).

Rnd 2: Turn; sk joining st, sl st in next ch st and then into ch-2 sp; ch 3, 2 dc in same sp; * ch 1, work (3 dc, ch 2, 3 dc) all in next ch-2 sp for corner; rep from * twice more; ch 1, 3 dc in beg corner sp (**Fig 3**); ch 2, join with a sl st in top of beg ch-3. Finish off, leaving approx 14" sewing length.

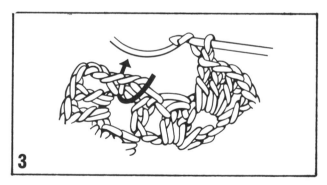

TWO-COLOR SQUARE

With first color listed for square (*center color*), ch 4, join with a sl st to form a ring.

Rnd 1 (wrong side): Ch 3, 2 dc in ring; * ch 2, 3 dc in ring; rep from * twice more; ch 2, join with a sl st in top of beg ch-3. Finish off center color, leaving approx 4" end to weave in now or later.

Rnd 2: Turn; join second color listed for square with a sl st in any ch-2 sp; ch 3, 2 dc in same sp; * ch 1, work (3 dc, ch 2, 3 dc) all in next ch-2 sp for corner; rep from * twice more; ch 1, 3 dc in beg corner sp; ch 2, join with a sl st in top of beg ch-3. Finish off, leaving approx 14" sewing length.

DIAGONAL TWO-COLOR SQUARE

> **NOTE**
> For "Color A", use either color listed for square; then use rem color for "Color B".

With Color A, ch 4, join with a sl st to form a ring.

Rnd 1 (wrong side): Ch 3, 2 dc in ring; ch 2, 3 dc in ring; drop Color A (*do not cut*); with Color B (*leave approx 4" end to weave in now or later*), ch 2 (**Fig 4**); continuing with Color B, work (3 dc in ring, ch 2) twice; join with a sl st in top of beg ch-3.

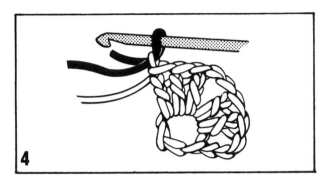

4

Rnd 2: Turn; sk joining st, sl st in next ch st and then into ch-2 sp; ch 3, 2 dc in same sp; ch 1, work (3 dc, ch 2, 3 dc) all in next ch-2 sp for corner; ch 1, 3 dc in next ch-2 sp, ch 2; finish off Color B, leaving approx 14" sewing length. With Color A, work 3 dc in same sp (*corner completed*); ch 1, work (3 dc, ch 2, 3 dc) all in next ch-2 sp for corner; ch 1, 3 dc in beg corner sp (*over sl sts of Color B*); ch 2, join with a sl st in top of beg ch-3. Finish off, leaving approx 14" sewing length.

JOINING SQUARES

> **NOTE**
> Arrange and join squares to form the "picture" following chart given with the individual afghan instructions.

To join, hold two squares with right sides tog, positioned (*whenever possible*) with sewing length in upper right-hand corner. Thread yarn (*use matching yarn when a sewing length is not available*) into tapestry or yarn needle. Carefully matching sts on both squares, beg with one corner st and sew with overcast st **in outer lps only** across side, ending with one st at next corner. Join squares in rows across and then sew these rows tog; or sew squares to form parts of the "picture", then sew these units tog. At each four-corner junction, either join all four corners securely, or if a small decorative opening is desired, do not join.

FREIGHT TRAIN

SIZE

54" × 72"

MATERIALS

DAWN SAYELLE* knitting worsted weight yarn:
    22 oz Baby Blue #312
    16 oz Nile Green #351
    12 oz Steel Gray #365
    8 oz Black #371
    6 oz each of:
        Lemon #331
        Blue #317A
    4 oz White #301
    3 oz Flame #325A
    2 oz each of:
        Forest Green #356
        Lilac #335
        Hot Pink #337
        Mulberry #324
    1 oz Hot Orange #340
Size G aluminum crochet hook (or size required for gauge)

GAUGE

One square = 2¼"

INSTRUCTIONS

Following Basic Picture Afghan Instructions, make and join the required number of One-Color, Two-Color and Diagonal Two-Color Squares as listed with the Train Chart.

When all squares have been made and joined, lightly steam press afghan on wrong side. Then make the following applique details and sew in place as indicated on Train Chart, using matching sewing thread.

WHEEL (make 16)

With Black, ch 8.

Row 1: Sc in 2nd ch from hook, dc in next ch; 2 tr in next ch, 2 double trc in next ch [*TO WORK DOUBLE TR: (YO hook) 3 times, insert hook in st and draw up a lp (5 lps now on hook); work (YO and draw through 2 lps on hook) 4 times: double tr made*]; 2 tr in next ch, dc in next ch, sc in last ch.

Row 2: Ch 1, turn; 2 sc in first sc, work (sc in next st, 2 sc in next st) twice; work (2 sc in next st, sc in next st) twice, 2 sc in last st: 16 sc.

Row 3: Ch 1, turn; sc in each sc across.

Row 4: Ch 1, turn; 2 sc in first sc, work (sc in next sc, 2 sc in next sc) 3 times; 2 sc in each of next 3 sc, work (sc in next sc, 2 sc in next sc) 3 times: 26 sc.

Row 5: Ch 1, turn; sc in each sc across. Finish off; weave in ends. Sew to afghan, having last row just worked facing afghan.

FULL HITCH (make 4)

With Black, make a chain to measure approx 4¼" long. Finish off; weave in ends. Sew to afghan, having wrong side of chain facing up.

HALF HITCH (make 6)

With Black, make a chain to measure approx 2½" long. Finish off; weave in ends. Sew to afghan, having wrong side of chain facing up.

DOOR OUTLINE (on blue car)

With Lemon, make two chains, each 8½" long for crossed diagonal outlines. Finish off; weave in ends. Sew to afghan, having wrong side of chains facing up. With Lemon, make another chain to measure approx 20" long for outline around door. Finish off and sew to afghan in same manner.

FREIGHT TRAIN CHART

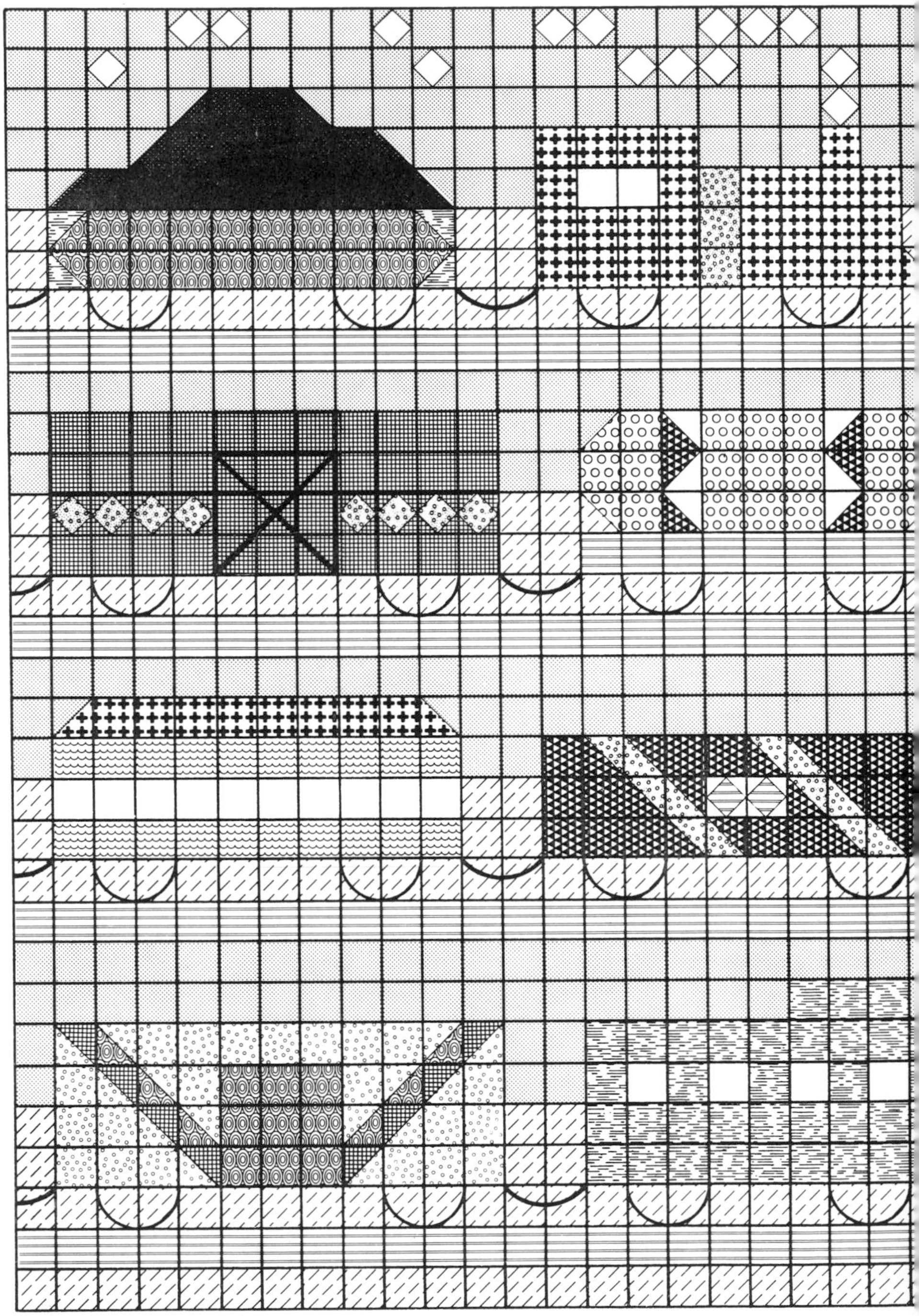

ONE-COLOR SQUARES

Color (number needed)

- Black (15)
- White (16)
- Forest Green (35)
- Baby Blue (197)
- Hot Pink (17)
- Flame (35)
- Lilac (25)
- Blue (36)
- Mulberry (16)
- Nile Green (153)
- Lemon (24)
- Hot Orange (20)
- Steel Gray (105)

DIAGONAL TWO-COLOR SQUARES

Colors (number needed)

- Forest Green/Baby Blue (2)
- Forest Green/Nile Green (1)
- Baby Blue/Black (6)
- Baby Blue/Hot Pink (2)
- Hot Pink/Nile Green (2)
- Lemon/Mulberry (12)
- Lemon/Blue (8)
- Lemon/Lilac (6)
- Mulberry/White (6)
- Flame/Lilac (4)

TWO-COLOR SQUARES

Colors (number needed)

- Baby Blue/White (15)
- White/Steel Gray (2)
- Blue/Lemon (8)

APPLIQUÉ DETAILS

- Wheels
- Full Hitch
- Half Hitch
- Door Outline

SILENT STAR

SIZE

49½" × 63"

MATERIALS

DAWN SAYELLE* knitting worsted weight yarn:
- 20 oz each of:
- Pink #363
- Nile Green #351
- 16 oz White #301
- 12 oz Primrose #309
- 4 oz Watermelon #325

Size G aluminum crochet hook (or size required for gauge)

GAUGE

One square = 2¼"

INSTRUCTIONS

Following Basic Picture Afghan Instructions, make and join the required number of One-Color and Diagonal Two-Color Squares as listed with the Silent Star Chart.

When all squares have been made and joined, lightly steam press afghan on wrong side.

SILENT STAR CHART

ONE COLOR SQUARES

Color (number needed)

Nile Green (136)

Pink (44)

White (48)

DIAGONAL TWO-COLOR SQUARES

Colors (number needed)

Nile Green/White (96)

Pink/Primrose (148)

Pink/White (96)

Watermelon/Primrose (48)

CHAPTER 3

RIPPLE AFGHANS
TO KNIT & CROCHET

Probably no other design is more beloved of knitters and crocheters than the ripple—sometimes called the chevron or zigzag pattern.

This design, with its gently undulating waves, lends itself to many different design approaches. We think you'll enjoy this group we've collected for you.

[CROCHETED]
YELLOW ROSE RIPPLE

Delightful floral motifs combined with ripple sections make up this colorful afghan. If you prefer, make it in a combination of rose, lavender, and blues with the Grass green

SIZE

45″ × 60″ before fringing

MATERIALS

DAWN SAYELLE* knitting worsted weight yarn:
14 oz Grass Green #357
12 oz each of
Lemon #331
White #301
Primrose #309
Light Gold #342
Antique Gold #344
Size H aluminum crochet hook (or size required for gauge)

GAUGE

One floral motif = 4″ square
In sc, 4 sts = 1″

INSTRUCTIONS

FLORAL MOTIF (make 12)

NOTE
All rnds are worked on right side.

With Lemon, ch 4, join with a sl st to form a ring.

Rnd 1: Work beg PC (*popcorn*) in ring as follows: Ch 3, work 3 dc in ring; drop lp from hook, insert hook in top of ch-3; hook dropped lp (**Fig 1**) and pull through st (*beg PC made*). ***** Ch 3, work PC in ring (**To make PC:** *Work 4 dc in ring; drop lp from hook, insert hook in top of first dc of 4-dc group just made; hook dropped lp and pull through st = PC made*); rep from ***** twice more. Ch 3, join with a sl st in top of ch-3 of beg PC : 4 ch-3 sps.

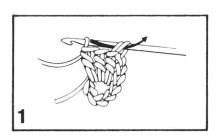

Rnd 2: ***** Sl st into next ch-3 sp, ch 4; rep from ***** 3 times more, join with a sl st in beg sl st : 4 ch-4 sps.

Rnd 3: Work (sc, hdc, 5 dc, hdc, sc) in next ch-4 sp for petal; rep from ***** 3 times more : 4 petals.

NOTE
Do not join rnd.

Rnd 4: *****Work BP (*Back post*) sl st around first sc of next petal (**To work BP sl st:** *Insert hook from back to front to back around post of st—see* **Fig 2**; *hook yarn and draw yarn back around st and through lp on hook = BP sl st made*), ch 4; sk next 3 sts, work BP sl st around next st (*center st*) of same petal, ch 4; rep from ***** 3 times more, join with a sl st in beg sl st : 8 ch-4 sps.

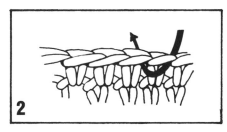

Rnd 5: ***** Work (sc, hdc, 3 dc, hdc, sc) in next ch-4 sp; rep from ***** 7 times more : 8 petals.

NOTE
Do not join rnd.

Rnd 6: ***** Work BP sl st around first sc of next petal, ch 3; rep from ***** 7 times more, join with a sl st in beg sl st : 8 ch-3 sps. Finish off Lemon.

61

Rnd 7: With right side facing, join Grass Green with a sl st in first ch-3 sp of prev rnd; ch 1, work (2 sc, 2 hdc, dc) in same sp as joining. * Ch 3 (*for corner*), work (dc, 2 hdc, 2 sc) in next ch-3 sp, work (2 sc, 2 hdc, dc) in next ch-3 sp; rep from * twice more. Ch 3 (*for last corner*), work (dc, 2 hdc, 2 sc) in last ch-3 sp; join with a sl st in beg sc.

Rnd 8: Ch 1, sc in same st as joining. * Sc in each st to corner ch-3 sp, work 3 sc in corner sp; rep from * 3 times more. Sc in each rem st along last side, join with a sl st in beg sc. Finish off Grass Green, leaving approx 4″ end for marker (*for working side ripple section later*). Weave in other yarn ends.

SIDE RIPPLE SECTION

NOTE
Afghan is worked lengthwise in two sections, with each section beginning at center and working outward—toward side edge.

Row 1 (joining motifs): Hold one floral motif with right side facing you and marked edge (*with yarn end*) across top. Join White with a sl st **in back lp** (*lp away from you*) of center sc of 3-sc group at upper right-hand corner. **Continue by working in back lp of each st as follows.** Ch 1, sc in same st as joining and in each of next 12 sc. * Work 3 sc in next sc (*center sc of 3-sc corner group*) for point; sc in each of next 11 sc, work dec (*decrease*) over next 2 sc (**To work DEC:** *Draw up a lp in each of next 2 sts, YO and draw through all 3 lps on hook*: dec made). Pick up next motif; hold motif with right side facing you and marked edge across top. Beg in center sc of 3-sc group at upper right-hand corner and work as follows (*remember to work in back lp of sts*). Dec over center sc of 3-sc corner group and next sc, sc in each of next 11 sc; rep from * to last point of last (*12th*) motif. Work 3 sc in next sc (*center sc of 3-sc corner group*) for last point; sc in each of next 12 sc, sc in next sc (*center sc of 3-sc corner group*).

Row 2 (ripple patt row): Ch 1, turn. **Working in back lp of each st**, sc in first sc, sk one sc, sc in each of next 12 sc. * Work 3 sc in next sc (*center sc of 3-sc group at point*), sc in each of next 12 sc; sk 2 sc, sc in each of next 12 sc; rep from * to last point. Work 3 sc in next sc (*center sc of 3-sc group at last point*), sc in each of next 12 sc; sk one sc, sc in last sc.

Finish off White, leaving approx 9″ end (*to be worked in later as part of fringe*). Then rep Row 2 in the following color sequence (*leaving approx 9″ ends when changing colors*): 2 rows each of Primrose, Light Gold, Antique Gold, Grass Green, Lemon and White (*12 rows total*).

Now rep prev 12-row color sequence 3 times more. Then for ending color sequence, work 2 rows each of Primrose, Light Gold, Antique Gold and Grass Green (*8 rows total*). Finish off.

OTHER SIDE RIPPLE SECTION

Row 1: Hold work with right side facing you and motifs across top. Working **in back lp of sts along motifs**, join White with a sl st in center sc of 3-sc group at upper right-hand corner (*where last st of first row of other section was worked*); ch 1, sc in same st as joining and in each of next 12 sc. * Work 3 sc in next sc (*center sc of 3-sc corner group*) for point; sc in each of next 11 sc, work dec over next sc and center sc of 3-sc corner group (*same st where dec was worked in first row of other section*). Working across edge of next motif, work dec over center sc of 3-sc corner group (*same st where dec was worked in first row of other section*) and next sc, sc in each of next 11 sc; rep from * to last point of last (*12th*) motif. Work 3 sc in next sc (*center sc of 3-sc corner group*) for last point, sc in each of next 12 sc, sc in next sc (*center sc of 3-sc corner group—same st where first sc of other section was worked*).

Complete section in same manner as other side ripple section.

FRINGE

Following Single Knot Fringe instructions on page 16, work fringe along each short end of afghan (*along end of rows*) as follows. Cut 16″ strands of each color. Use 4 strands of one color for each knot of fringe. Tie one matching knot at center (*Grass Green*) and one matching knot at each remaining color across (*be sure to work each knot of fringe 2 strands in from edge of afghan*), working in yarn ends as part of fringe.

[KNITTED]
FEATHER AND FAN

This is an old favorite traditional pattern, which is easy to knit yet beautiful. Worked on size 10 needles, it has a light, lacey look.

SIZE

48" × 64" before fringing.

MATERIALS

Mohair type worsted weight yarn: CARON
 DAZZLEAIRE:
    21 oz Off White #2615
36" long size 10 circular needle (or size required
    for gauge)

GAUGE

Each fan point = 4½"

INSTRUCTIONS

Loosely cast on 192 sts; do not join, work back and forth in rows.

Row 1: Knit.

Row 2: (K 2 tog) 4 times; (YO, K 1) 8 times; ***** (K 2 tog) 8 times; (YO, K 1) 8 times; rep from ***** 6 times; then (K 2 tog) 4 times.

Row 3: Knit.

Row 4: Purl.

Repeat these four rows for pattern; work until piece measures about 64", ending by working Row 4. Bind off loosely.

FRINGE

Follow Single Knot Fringe instructions on page 16. Cut strands 16" long and use 2 strands in each knot. Tie 4 knots in YOs center of each panel at each short end; tie 2 knots in outer corner panels.

[KNITTED]
PRIMROSE CABLES

The yellow of primroses, the blue of the spring sky are combined in this afghan. Ombre yarn alternates with solid color cable panels for an unusually beautiful effect.

SIZE

41″ × 54″ before fringing

MATERIALS

Mohair type worsted weight yarn, CARON
   DAZZELAIRE:
      12 oz Pale Yellow #2635
       6 oz Sky Blue #2620
      18 oz Sundance (ombre) #2675
14″ size 10 straight needle   (or sizes required for gauge)
Size G aluminum crochet hook for joining panels
Cable stitch holder or double point needle

GAUGE

For ombre panel, 20 sts = 3¾″ before assembling

NOTE
A YO loop begins every row; for ease in counting loops and assembling panels, tie a marker of contrasting yarn every 25th loop on each side of panel. Mark cast-on row of each panel as panel bottom.

INSTRUCTIONS

SUNDANCE OMBRE PANEL *(make 4)*

Cast on 20 sts.

Row 1: YO, K 7, K 2 tog, K 11.

Repeat Row 1 until there are 150 YO loops on each side of the panel. Bind off loosely.

CABLE PANEL *(make 2 in Pale Yellow; make 1 in Sky Blue)*

Cast on 41 sts.

Row 1 (cable twist row): YO, K 7, K 2 tog, K 3; sl next 4 sts onto cable needle and hold in *back* of work; K 4, K 4 sts from cable needle, K 3, sl 4 sts onto cable needle and hold in *back* of work; K 4, K 4 sts from cable needle, K 11.

Row 2: YO, K 7, K 2 tog; K 2, P 8, K 3; P 8, K 11.

Row 3: YO, K 7, K 2 tog, K 30.

Rows 4–9: Rep Rows 2 and 3, 3 more times.

Row 10: Rep Row 2.

Repeat these 10 rows until there are 150 YO loops on each side of the panel, ending by working Row 10.

Bind-Off Row: Bind off 7 sts; K 2 tog, bind off the K 2 tog; * place next 4 sts on cable needle, bind off 4 sts; bind off 4 sts on cable needle; bind off 3 sts; rep from * to last 11 sts, bind off.

JOINING

Join panels with crochet hook, as follows: Place Sky Blue cable panel with wrong side facing wrong side of a Sundance Ombre panel and cast-on rows at bottom; join Sky Blue yarn with an sc working through both bottom YO loops; continue working sc to join YO loops, adjusting tension to keep work flat. Work to top of panels, finish off. Join another ombre panel to other side of Sky Blue panel in same manner. Using Pale Yellow yarn, join a yellow panel to each of the joined ombre panels, in same manner. Then using Pale Yellow yarn, join remaining ombre panels, one to each side of yellow panels. Weave in all loose ends.

FRINGE

Follow Single Knot Fringe instructions on page 16. Cut strands 16″ long in all colors. Working across each short end of afghan, knot 1 strand in each st across, matching fringe color to panel color.

[CROCHETED]
GOLDEN SUNRISE

This cheerful yellow afghan makes you feel good just to look at it—and it's a delight to snuggle up under. Done in an easy double crochet stitch, the design is a showcase for your favorite color yarn.

SIZE

45″ × 60″

MATERIALS

Worsted weight yarn:
   35 oz Yellow
Size J aluminum crochet hook (or size required for gauge)

GAUGE

3 dc = 1″

INSTRUCTIONS

Ch 189 loosely.

Foundation Row: Sc in 2nd ch from hook, sc in next ch, sk next ch; * sc in each of next 10 chs, 3 sc in next ch; sc in each of next 10 chs, † sk next 2 chs*; rep from * to * 6 times, then rep from * to † once, sk next ch, sc in each of last 2 chs, ch 3, turn.

Pattern Row:

> **NOTE**
> Throughout Pattern, ch 3 counts as a st; work in **back loop only** of each stitch from now on.

Dc in next st, sk 1 st; * dc in each of next 10 sts, 3 dc in next st, dc in each of next 10 sts; † sk 2 sts*; rep from * to * 6 times; then rep from * to † once, sk 1 st, dc in each of last 2 sts, ch 3, turn.

Repeat Pattern Row until work measures 60″ long, end final Pattern Row with ch 1, turn.

Last Row: Sc in first 2 sts, sk 1 st; * sc in each of next 10 sts, 3 sc in next st, sc in each of next 10 sts; † sk 2 sts; * rep from * to * 6 times, then rep from * to † once, sk 1 st, sc in each of last 2 sts, finish off.

Weave in all yarn ends. Lightly steam side edges if needed to keep from curling.

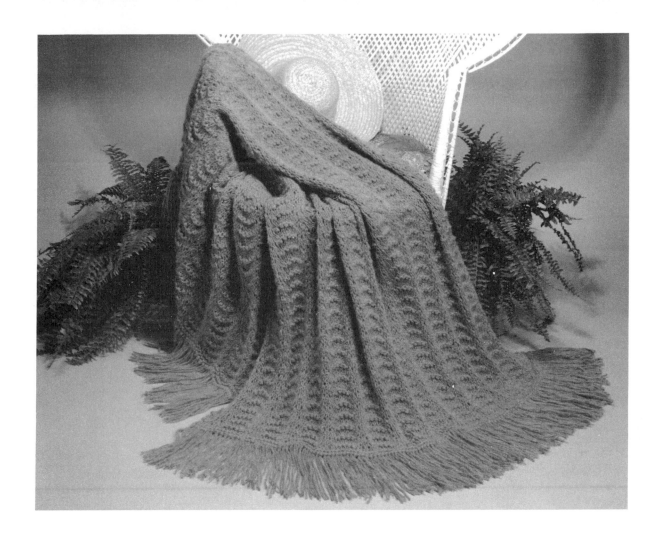

[KNITTED]
BLUE LACE

What could be easier than this 4-row pattern? And on a size 11 needle, it's fast, too. The pretty rippling effect has a lacey look you'll love.

SIZE

40″ × 54″ before fringing

MATERIALS

Mohair type knitting worsted weight yarn, CARON DAZZLEAIRE:
   24 oz Slate Blue #2812
36″ long size 11 circular needle (or size required for gauge)

GAUGE

11 sts = 3½″; 8 rows = 2½″

INSTRUCTIONS

Cast on 143 sts.; do not join, work back and forth in rows.

Row 1: Knit.

Row 2: Purl.

Row 3: * (P2 tog) twice; (inc 1, K1) 3 times [to inc, pick up bar before next st]; inc 1, (p2 tog) twice; repeat from * across.

Row 4: Purl.

Repeat these 4 rows for pattern until afghan measures 54″, ending by working row 4. Bind off in purl st.

FRINGE

Follow Single Knot Fringe Instructions on page 16. Cut strands 16″ and use one strand for each knot. Tie knot through every other stitch across each short end of afghan.

[CROCHETED]
BROWN SHADED RIPPLE

This is a very easy ripple, worked with a K hook in shades of beige, brown, black and fisherman, spiced with cinnamon. Vary the colors to match your own decor.

SIZE

42″ × 62″

MATERIALS

DAWN SAYELLE* knitting worsted weight yarn:
  12 oz each of:
    Black #371
    Chocolate Brown #306A
    Cinnamon #307A
    Honey Beige #303
    Fisherman #336
Size K aluminum crochet hook (or size required for gauge)

GAUGE

In pattern stitch, 2 shells = 1½″

INSTRUCTIONS

With Black, ch 342 LOOSELY.

Row 1 (foundation row): Sc in 2nd ch from hook; sk one ch, work (sc, ch 2, sc) in next ch (**shell made**); work (sk 2 chs, shell in next ch) 4 times. * Sk 2 chs, work (shell, ch 3, shell) all in next ch for point; work (sk 2 chs, shell in next ch) 4 times; sk 2 chs, sc in next ch; sk 3 chs, sc in next ch; work (sk 2 chs, shell in next ch) 4 times; rep from * 8 times more. Sk 2 chs, work (shell, ch 3, shell) all in next ch for last point; work (sk 2 chs, shell in next ch) 5 times; sk one ch, dc in last ch.

Row 2 (patt row): Ch 1, turn; sc in dc, sc in ch-2 sp of first shell; work shell in ch-2 sp in each of next 5 shells. * Work (shell, ch 3, shell) in ch-3 sp at point, work shell in ch-2 sp in each of next 4 shells; sc in ch-2 sp of next shell, sk 2 sc, sc in ch-2 sp of next shell; work shell in ch-2 sp in each of next 4 shells; rep from * to last point. Work (shell, ch 3, shell) in ch-3 sp at last point, work shell in ch-2 sp in each of next 5 shells; sc in ch-2 sp of last shell, dc in last sc.

Rep Row 2 in the following color sequece: 2 rows each of Chocolate Brown, Cinnamon, Honey Beige, Fisherman and Black (*10 rows total*).

NOTE

TO CHANGE COLORS, work last st of row until 2 lps rem on hook; cut old color leaving 4″ end. With new color (leave 4″ end), complete st (YO and draw through both lps on hook): color changed. Then work several sts over yarn ends at beg of next row.

Now rep prev 10-row color sequence, 7 times more. Finish off; weave in all ends.

[CROCHETED]

OCEAN WAVES

The lovely colors and wave-like pattern of this afghan remind us of the ocean. And you'll have oceans of fun making it quickly in double crochet on a J hook.

SIZE

50" × 60"

MATERIALS

COATS & CLARK RED HEART® 4-ply handknitting yarn, Art. E. 267:
  24 oz Dk Turquoise #515 Color A
  12 oz Nile Green #679 Color B
  8 oz White #1 Color C
Size J aluminum crochet hook (or size required for gauge)

GAUGE

7 sts = 2"
4 rows = 2¼"

INSTRUCTIONS

Starting at narrow edge with Color A, ch 170.

Row 1: Draw up a loop in 2nd and 3rd chs from hook, YO and draw through all 3 loops on hook—1 sc decreased; * sc in next 10 chs, 3 sc in next ch, sc in next 10 chs, draw up a loop in each of next 3 chs, YO and draw through all 4 loops on hook; repeat from * 5 more times; sc in next 10 chs, 3 sc in next ch, sc in next 10 chs, draw up a loop in each of last 2 chs and complete a sc: 169 sts; ch 3, turn.

Row 2: Skip first st, dc in next 11 sts; * 3 dc in next st, dc in next 10 sts; holding back on hook the last loop of each dc, dc in next 3 sts, YO and draw through all loops on hook; dc in next 10 sts; repeat from * 5 more times; 3 dc in next st, dc in next 10 sts; holding back on hook the last loop of each dc, dc in each of last 2 sts, YO and draw through all loops on hook—1 dc decreased; ch 3, turn.

Row 3: Working in **back loop only** of each st, work as for Row 2 to within last 2 dc (do not count ch-3 as 1 dc), dec 1 dc over last 2 sts, do not work in top of ch-3; ch 3, turn.

Row 4: Working through both loops of each dc, work as for Row 2 to within last 2 dc, dec 1 dc over last 2 dc (do not work in top of ch-3); ch 3, turn.

Repeating Rows 3 and 4 for pattern, work in pattern in the following color sequence:

  * 2 rows Color A
  2 rows Color C
  4 rows Color A
  2 rows Color C
  6 rows Color A
  6 rows Color B
  4 rows Color A
  6 rows Color B
  6 rows Color A

Repeat from * once; then work:
  2 rows Color C
  4 rows Color A
  2 rows Color C
  5 rows Color A

At end of last row, ch 1, turn.

Last Row: Continuing with Color A, dec 1 sc over first 2 dc; sc in next 10 dc; *3 sc in next dc, sc in next 10 dc; dec 2 sc over next 3 dc, sc in next 10 dc; rep from * 5 more times; 3 sc in next sc, sc in next 10 dc, dec 2 sc over last 2 sts. Finish off.

Weave in all yarn ends.

[CROCHETED]
BLAZING SUNSET

The glowing colors of the yarns used in this afghan create excitement—and who could be chilly under this on a cold winter night? For a completely different look, substitute soft, pastel shades.

SIZE

43″ × 60″ before fringing

MATERIALS

COATS & CLARK RED HEART® 4-ply handknitting
    yarn, Art. E 267:
        7 oz each of:
            Vermillion #921
            Jockey Red #902
            Scarlet #909
            Burnt Orange #255
            Tangerine #253
            Orange #245
            Yellow #230
            Maize #261
Size J aluminum crochet hook (or size required for
    gauge)

GAUGE

19 sts = 4½″; 8 rows = 3″

NOTE

To change color at end of row, draw up loop in last st (2 loops on hook), change to new color, YO, draw through both loops, ch 1, turn.

INSTRUCTIONS

With Vermillion loosely ch 200.

Row 1: Sc in 2nd ch from hook, sc in each of the next 3 chs; * sc 3 times in next ch (inc made), sc in next 8 chs, skip 2 chs (dec made), sc in next 8 chs.

Repeat from * 10 times, ending sc 3 times in next ch, sc in each of last 4 chs; ch 1, turn.

Row 2: Working in *back loop* only of each st, skip first 2 sts, sc in each of next 3 sc, * sc 3 times in next sc (center stitch of point), sc in each of next 8 sc, skip 2 sc, sc in each of next 8 sc.

Repeat from * across, ending sc 3 times in next sc, sc in each of next 3 sc, skip last 2 sc, sc in turning ch-1; ch 1, turn.

Repeat Row 2, 8 more times (10 rows Vermillion). Attach Jockey Red to last st of Row 10. Cut old color leaving a 4″ yarn end for weaving later.

Repeat Row 2 in Jockey Red for 10 rows. Attach Scarlet, repeat Row 2 for 10 rows. Continue to repeat Row 2, keeping color sequence as follows; 10 rows each of Burnt Orange, Tangerine, Orange, Yellow and Maize. Afghan is now half done. Complete rest of afghan by reversing the 10-row color sequence.

Weave in all loose ends.

FRINGE

Follow Single Knot Fringe Instructions on page 16. With Vermillion, cut 16″ strands and use 6 strands in each knot. Tie knots at the points across each short end of afghan.

QUICK CROCHETS

This collection of 14 afghans should delight the heart of any crocheter. From lacey to tailored, from palest pastels to brightest brights, these afghans are as beautiful as they are quick and easy to make. They're made with big hooks, and some with two strands of yarn worked together. The colorful designs include an innovative "checkerboard" afghan, one that is woven through a background mesh, and a fisherman style.

PINK PERFECTION

This is an extra easy design, perfect for the beginner. You can change the color scheme: make it in shades of blue with lilac; beiges and oranges; or use six bright and bold different shades for a striking effect.

SIZE

42½″ × 75″ before fringing

MATERIALS

COATS & CLARK RED HEART® 4-ply Handknitting Yarn, Art. E. 267:
  3½ oz White
  10½ oz each of:
    Lt, Med and Dk Pink
    Lt, Med and Dk Raspberry
    (or any six colors of your choice)
Size K aluminum crochet hook (or size required for gauge)

GAUGE

With two strands of yarn, 5 tr = 2″; 2 rows = 2½″

NOTE
Work with 2 strands of yarn throughout.

INSTRUCTIONS

STRIP *(make 1 strip in each of the 6 colors)*

Starting at narrow edge, with two yarn strands held together, ch 110.

Row 1 (right side): Tr in 5th ch from hook and in each ch across: 107 tr, counting ch-4 as a tr; ch 4, turn.

Rows 2–9: Skip first tr, tr in **back loop only** of each tr across, tr in top of turning ch; ch 4, turn. At end of last row, omit ch 4, finish off.

JOINING

Hold Row 9 of Lt Pink and starting ch of Med Pink strips together, with wrong sides facing. With 2 strands of white, working through both strips, sc in each st across long edge; fasten off. In same manner, join remaining strips in this order: Dk Pink, Lt, Med and Dk Raspberry.

FRINGE

Following instructions for Single Knot Fringe on page 16, cut white strands 18″ long. Use 4 strands, folded in half, for each knot. Knot fringe in every other stitch along each narrow edge, and in end st of every row and between rows along each long edge.

RIPPLING SHELLS

A big wooden crochet hook, size L, makes these shells grow quickly under your flying fingers. Need a gift in a hurry? Then this is an afghan to choose. Try it also in a solid color.

SIZE

40″ × 54″

MATERIALS

Mohair type worsted weight yarn, CARON DAZZLEAIRE:
- 12 oz Wheat #2823 Color A
- 12 oz Golden Delicious #2825 Color B
- 12 oz Vanilla #2822 Color C
- 12 oz Cinnamon #2824 Color D

Size L wooden crochet hook (or size required for gauge)

GAUGE

2 shells = 5″, 4 rows = 3″

NOTES

1. To change color at end of row, work across row, YO, draw up a loop in last st (3 loops on hook); YO, draw through 2 loops; change to new color, YO, draw through remaining 2 loops.
2. When fastening off old color and attaching new, leave an 8″ yarn end to be used later in fringe.

INSTRUCTIONS

With Color A, chain 148 loosely.

Row 1: 2 dc in 4th ch from hook, * skip 2 ch, 1 sc in next ch, skip 2 ch, 5 dc in next ch (shell made); repeat from * ending 3 dc in last ch; ch 1, turn.

Row 2: 1 sc in first dc, * 5 dc in next sc, 1 sc in center dc of next shell; repeat from * ending 1 sc in top of turning ch; ch 3, turn.

Row 3: 2 dc in first sc, * 1 sc in center dc of next shell, 5 dc in next sc; repeat from * ending 3 dc in last sc; ch 1, turn.

Row 4: Repeat Row 2; attach Color B in last st. Fasten off A, ch 3, turn.

Rows 5–8: With Color B, repeat Rows 3 & 2 for 4 rows, changing to Color C on last stitch of Row 8; ch 3, turn.

Rows 9–12: With Color C, repeat Rows 3 & 2 for 4 rows, changing to color D on last stitch of Row 12; ch 3, turn.

Rows 13–16: With Color D, repeat Rows 3 & 2 for 4 rows, changing to Color A on last stitch of Row 16; ch 3, turn.

Repeat Rows 1–16, 4 times. With Color A, repeat Rows 1–4 once.

Weave in all loose ends other than the ends reserved for fringe.

FRINGE

Follow Single Knot Fringe Instructions on page 16. Cut 50 strands of colors B, C & D and 60 strands of Color A, each 16″ long. Folding each strand in half for each knot fringe, tie knot through each stitch of matching color across each short end of afghan. 5 knots are worked in each color segment. Include the extra yarn ends into that particular colored knot.

CARAMELS AND CREAM

Fun to make cross stitches are combined with double crochet in this afghan, which combines an ombre with a solid color. You could also use two solid colors, or make it entirely in one solid shade.

SIZE

44" × 54" before fringing

MATERIALS

Worsted weight yarn:
    24 oz Earthtone ombre Color A
    8 oz Cream Color B
Size J aluminum crochet hook (or size required for gauge)

GAUGE

5 dc = 2"; 3 rows = 2"

NOTE

When changing colors, YO, draw up a loop in last stitch (3 loops on hook) YO, draw through 2 loops; CHANGE TO NEW COLOR, YO, draw through remaining loops.

INSTRUCTIONS

With Color B, chain 119 loosely.

Row 1: Dc in 3rd ch from hook and in each ch across; ch 2, turn.

Row 2: Dc in each dc across and in ch-2 turning chain; ch 2, turn.

Rows 3–6: Repeat Row 2, attaching Color A on last st of row 6; ch 2, turn.

Rows 7–16: Repeat Row 2 in Color A for 10 rows, attaching Color B on last stitch of Row 16; ch 2, turn.

Row 17: With Color B, dc in 3rd dc, dc in 2nd dc (creating a cross stitch). * Skip dc already used plus 2 more dc, work another cross st pattern; repeat from * across ending with a dc in turning ch; ch 2, turn.

Row 18: Repeat Row 17.

Row 19: Repeat Row 17, attaching Color A on last stitch; ch 2, turn.

Repeat Rows 7–19, 5 times. Repeat Rows 1–16 one more time. Attach Color B, work 6 rows in dc. Fasten off.

FRINGE

Follow Single Knot Fringe Instructions on page 16. With Color A, cut strands 16" in length. Working across each short end of afghan, using 2 strands, folded in half, make a knot in each stitch across.

CHECKERBOARD

Bright and bold colors and an unusual design make this a perfect afghan for a teenager—or a swinging bachelor!

SIZE

44″ × 54″

MATERIALS

Worsted weight yarn:
   8 oz Black
   7 oz White
   21 oz Red
Size J aluminum crochet hook (or size required for gauge)

GAUGE

3 dc = 1″; 3 rows dc = 2″

NOTES
1. In carrying colors from one block to another, work over the yarn being carried.
2. To change colors, YO and draw up a loop in last stitch (3 loops on hook); YO, draw through 2 loops, **CHANGE TO NEW COLOR**, YO, draw through remaining 2 loops.

INSTRUCTIONS

With Black, chain 138 loosely.

Row 1: 1 dc in 3rd ch from hook and in each ch to end; drop Black and join Red; ch 3, turn (ch-3 counts as 1 dc).

Row 2: With Red, skip first dc, dc in each dc across; change to Black, ch 3, turn.

Row 3: Skip first dc, 1 dc in each of next 3 dc; * attach white, work 1 dc in each of next 4 dc. Pick up Black, 1 dc in next 4 dc; Repeat from * across row ending with White in last 4 dc; ch 3, turn.

Row 4: Repeat Row 3, having White over White and Black over Black. On last White dc stitch, change to Black; ch 3, turn.

Row 5: Repeat Row 3, having Black over White and White over Black.

Row 6: Repeat Row 4. On last Black stitch, change to White; ch 3, turn.

Row 7: Repeat Row 3.

Row 8: Repeat Row 4.

Row 9: Repeat Row 5.

Row 10: Repeat Row 6. On last White stitch change to Red; ch 3, turn.

Row 11: With Red, skip 1st dc, dc in each dc across. Change to Black, ch 3, turn.

Row 12: With Black, skip first dc, dc in each dc across, change to Red, ch 3, turn.

Work 59 rows in Red, working a dc in each dc across the row, chaining 3 at the end of each row before turning. Afghan should measure approx 46″. At end of last row, attach Black, ch 3, turn.

Row 72: With Black, dc in each dc across; attach Red, ch 3, turn.

Row 73: With Red, dc in each dc across; attach White, ch 3, turn.

Rows 74–81: Repeat the checkerboard pattern as in the beginning, starting with Black. On last white dc stitch of Row 81, change to Red, ch 3, turn.

Row 82: Repeat Row 11.

Row 83: Repeat Row 12; *do not change to red or fasten off*, ch 2, turn.

FINISHING

With Black, ch 1, work 1 row of sc all around afghan, working 3 sc in each corner st and working 2 sc in each of the ch-3 turning stitches.

Weave in all loose ends.

SUMMER SKIES

Soft as a blue summer sky is this easy afghan, worked up quickly on a big wood crochet hook Size M. Double yarn throughout makes it double quick to crochet.

SIZE

42″ × 54″ before fringing

MATERIALS

Mohair type worsted weight yarn, CARON DAZZLEAIRE:
    18 oz White #2601 Color A
    12 oz Blues #2662 Color B
Size M wood crochet hook (or size required for gauge)

GAUGE

2 dc = 1″

NOTES

1. Yarn is worked **double** throughout.
2. To change color at end of rows: work across, YO, draw up a loop in last st (3 loops on hook); YO, draw through 2 loops; change to new color, YO, draw through remaining 2 loops; ch 2, turn.
3. Ch 2 at end of each row counts as first dc of next row.

PATTERN ROWS

There are two pattern rows, which are worked as follows:

Double Crochet Rows: Sk first dc, dc in next dc and in each dc across; dc *under* ch-2; ch 2, turn.

Cross Stitch Rows: Sk first dc, dc in next dc; * sk next dc, dc in next dc, dc in skipped dc (cross stitch made); rep from * across, ending dc in last dc, dc under ch-2; you should have 39 cross stitches with 2 dc at each end; ch 2, turn.

INSTRUCTIONS

With 2 strands of Color B, loosely ch 84 sts.

Foundation Row: Dc in 4th ch from hook and in each ch across; ch 2, turn.

Continue, always with two strands of yarn, working in the following color and row sequence:

With Color B: * 2 rows Double Crochet
           1 row Cross Stitch
           4 rows Double Crochet
           1 row Cross Stitch *
           1 row Double Crochet
           Repeat from * to * once more

With Color A: 3 rows Double Crochet
With Color B: 1 row Cross Stitch
With Color A: 4 rows Double Crochet
With Color B: 1 row Cross Stitch
With Color A: 3 rows Double Crochet
With Color B: 1 row Cross Stitch
With Color A: 4 rows Double Crochet

Afghan is now half completed. For second half, work the pattern and color sequence in reverse:

With Color B: 1 row Cross Stitch
With Color A: 3 rows Double Crochet
With Color B: 1 row Cross Stitch
With Color A: 4 rows Double Crochet
With Color B: 1 row Cross Stitch
With Color A: 3 rows Double Crochet
With Color B: 1 row Cross Stitch
           4 rows Double Crochet
           1 row Cross Stitch
           3 rows Double Crochet
           1 row Cross Stitch
           4 rows Double Crochet
           1 row Cross Stitch
           3 rows Double Crochet

Finish off, weave in all loose ends.

FRINGE

Follow Single Knot Fringe Instructions on page 16. Cut 168 strands, 16″ long in each color. Use 4 strands of White folded in half, for each knot and tie knot thru EVERY FOURTH stitch across each short end of afghan. With Blues, tie knots in between the White knots (knots are now tied into every other stitch).

DESERT SANDS

A beautiful ombre creates its own patterns in this easy afghan. Try it in a solid color for a completely different look. A size K hook and open mesh rows make it lightweight and fast to make.

SIZE

41" × 58"

MATERIALS

Mohair type worsted weight yarn CARON DAZZLEAIRE:
    24 oz Navaho (ombre) #2618
Size K aluminum crochet hook (or size required for gauge)

GAUGE

4 dc = 1"

INSTRUCTIONS

Chain 200 loosely.

Row 1: Dc in 4th ch from hook, and in each ch across: 198 dc counting turning chain; ch 3, turn.

Row 2: Dc in next st, * ch 1, skip 1 dc, dc in next dc; Repeat from * ending dc in end st; ch 3, turn.

Row 3: Dc in next st, * ch 1, skip ch-1 sp, dc in next dc; Repeat from * ending dc in end st; ch 3, turn.

Rows 4–5: Repeat Row 3.

Row 6: Dc in each st and ch-1 space; ch 3, turn.

Row 7: Repeat Row 2.

Row 8: Repeat Row 3.

Row 9: Repeat Row 4.

Row 10: Repeat Row 5.

Repeat Rows 6–10 for pattern until piece measures about 41" from starting ch, ending by working Row 6.

FRINGE

Follow Single Knot Fringe on page 16. Cut strands 16" long. Use 2 strands, folded in half and tie knot around each ch-3 bar across each short end of afghan.

BEAUTIFUL BOBBLES

Bobbles are fun to do and work up quickly, giving a lovely textured effect. The beautiful, soft yarn makes the afghan drape gracefully.

SIZE

40" × 54" before fringing

MATERIALS

Mohair type worsted weight yarn, CARON DAZZLEAIRE:
   30 oz. Vanilla #2822
Size K aluminum crochet hook (or size required for gauge)

GAUGE

6 dc = 2½"; 4 pattern rows = 2½"

INSTRUCTIONS

Chain 128 sts loosely.

Foundation Row: Dc in 3rd chain from hook and in each ch across: 126 dc counting ch-2 as a dc; ch 1, turn.

Row 1 (wrong side): sc in first dc, skip 1 dc, * sc in 1 dc; (YO and draw up a loop in same dc where last sc was made) 3 times, YO and draw through 6 loops, YO and draw through remaining 2 loops (Bobble made). Skip 1 dc and push Bobble to back. Repeat from * to last dc and ch-2, make sc and Bobble in next dc, dc in top of ch-3: 62 Bobbles made; ch 1, turn.

Row 2: Sc in first dc, skip next Bobble; * in next sc, make sc and Bobble, skip next Bobble and push Bobble to the front. Repeat from * to last sc. Dc in last sc, ch 2, turn.

Row 3: Dc in next Bobble and in each st across, ch 2, turn.

Row 4: Dc in next dc and in each dc across; dc in top of ch-2; ch 1, turn.

Repeat rows 1–4 until afghan measures approx 40", ending by working Row 4. Fasten off. Weave in all loose ends.

FRINGE

Follow Single Knot Fringe Instructions on page 16. Cut strands 16" long. Use 4 strands, folded in half, and tie knot around the ch-2 of the 2 Bobble rows across each short end of afghan, plus a knot at the beg and ending dc rows (34 knots each side).

LEMON-LIME STRIPE

Fresh summer colors create this striking afghan, worked in an unusual pattern stitch. It's fun to make, and you can of course vary the color combinations. Try it in red, white and green for a Christmas afghan.

SIZE

46" × 64"

MATERIALS

Worsted weight yarn:
    18 oz each of:
        White
        Lemon Yellow
        Lime Green
Size I aluminum crochet hook (or size required for gauge)

GAUGE

6 sc = 2"

INSTRUCTIONS

BORDER

With white, ch 122.

Row 1: Sc in 2nd ch from hook and in each ch across; ch 1, turn.

Rows 2, 3 and 4: Sc across, ch 1, turn; in last sc of Row 4, draw up yellow through last loop, finish off white.

PATTERN

In this pattern you will be working single crochet stitches at base of stitches 2 or 3 rows below; this gives a decorative shell effect.

Row 1: Sc in first sc; * sc at base of next sc; sc at base of next sc *2 rows below*; sc at base of next sc *3 rows below*; sc at base of next sc *2 rows below*; sc at base of next sc; sc in next sc; rep from * across, ending sc in last sc, ch 1, turn.

Rows 2, 3 and 4: Sc in each sc across, ch 1, turn; at end of Row 4, draw up green, end off yellow.

Repeat Pattern Rows 1 through 4, drawing up white through last st in Pattern Row 4.

Repeat Pattern Rows 1 through 4, changing colors in sequence, white, yellow, green, 23 times; finish off, weave in all loose ends.

DIAGONAL CHEVRONS

This afghan is self-fringing—you make the fringe as you crochet each row. To create the textured pattern, double crochet stitches are worked in a slanting pattern.

SIZE

44″ × 54″

MATERIALS

Worsted weight yarn:
    12 oz Cream Color A   14 oz Camel Color D
     7 oz Gray Color B   3½ oz Orange Color E
    10½ oz Cocoa Color C

Size J aluminum crochet hook (or size required for gauge)

GAUGE

8 sc = 2"; 8 rows = 2½"

NOTES

This is an unusual afghan—you make the fringe as you work, by leaving a 7" end of yarn at the beginning and end of each row. **The afghan is worked entirely from the front side**, so be sure never to turn the work. Here are some techniques you will want to refer to as you work:

1. All sc stitches are worked in the **back loop only of each** stitch. This is the loop **away** from you.
2. All dc stitches are worked in the **front loop** of the sc stitch in the **second row below.**
3. From Row 2 on, begin every row like this: Leaving a 7" end of yarn, make a slip knot on hook; remove hook, insert it in **first st of previous row**, put slip knot back on hook and pull loop through, ch 1. **This counts as first st of the row.** This method gives a firm selvage edge.
4. **To end each row**, after working last st, cut yarn 7" from hook, pull yarn end through loop.
   Remember that each row is worked from the front; and that the yarn is begun and ended anew each row.

COLOR SEQUENCE

Work following pattern in this color sequence:

> * 2 rows Color A
> 4 rows Color B
> 2 rows Color A
> 6 rows Color C
> 2 rows Color A
> 8 rows Color D
> 2 rows Color A
> 6 rows Color E
> 2 rows Color A
> 8 rows Color D
> 2 rows Color A
> 6 rows Color C
> 2 rows Color A
> 4 rows Color B

Repeat Color Sequence from * 3 times, then work 2 more rows in Color A.

Color sequence is not mentioned in pattern; be sure to make the color changes as above.

INSTRUCTIONS

With Color A, make a slip knot on hook, leaving a 7" end; ch 186 loosely.

Row 1: Sc in 2nd from hook and in each ch across; fasten off, leaving a 7" end.

Rows 2 and 3: Join yarn in first st (Note 3 above); sc in **back loop** only of each st across; end off yarn (Note 4 above). *Joining and ending methods will not be mentioned again. Be sure to make color changes as you work, and to work in back loop only of each Single Crochet Stitch.*

Row 4: Join yarn in first sc, sc in next sc; sk next sc, work dc in front loop of sc 2 rows below; * sc in next 9 sc, sk next sc, dc as before in 2nd row below; repeat from * across, ending with 2 sc.

Row 5: Join yarn in first sc, sc in next 2 sc, sk 1 sc, dc as before; * work 9 sc, dc as before; repeat from * across ending with 3 sc.

Rows 6–13: Repeat Row 5, but add 1 more sc at beginning of each row before working the first dc. This moves all the dc stitches over one space on each row, placing them on a diagonal.

Row 14: Repeat Row 4.

Row 15: Repeat Row 5.

Rows 16–23: Repeat Rows 6–13.

Row 24: Repeat Row 4.

Repeat these 24 rows for pattern (working Row 1 now into sc sts instead of into starting chains), following the color sequence.

At end, with **wrong side** of afghan facing, and working over last row completed, join Color A and work 1 row of sc in each stitch across that end of afghan. Fasten off. With **right side** of afghan facing and working over starting chain, join Color A and sc in each ch across. Fasten off. Trim fringe evenly.

MULTI-COLOR STRIPED DELIGHT

For lovers of single crochet, this is a true delight. Try your own color combinations—soft pastels or bright shades will completely change the look. In our colors, its a nice gift for a man.

SIZE

44″ × 54″ before fringing

MATERIALS

Worsted weight yarn:
- 20 oz Dark Brown Color A
- 12 oz Medium Brown Color B
- 4 oz Beige Color C
- 8 oz Gold Color D
- 8 oz Fisherman Color E

Size J aluminum crochet hook (or size required for gauge)

GAUGE

10 sts = 2½″; 15 rows (1 complete pattern) = 7½″

NOTES

1. In starting and ending each new color sequence, leave an 8″ yarn end. These will be used later as part of the fringe.
2. When changing colors, pull new color through last 2 loops to complete sc.

INSTRUCTIONS

Using Color A, chain 200.

Row 1 (right side): Sc in 2nd ch from hook; * ch 1, skip 1 ch, sc in next ch repeat from * across, ch 1, turn.

Row 2: Sc in first sc; * ch 1, skip ch-1 space, sc in next sc; repeat from * across, ch 1, turn.

Repeat Row 2 only for pattern, always working ch-1 over a ch-1 space and sc over sc.

Attach color B and work in stripe pattern as follows:
2 rows each of A, B, E, B, C.
4 rows of A
1 row of D

Repeat these 15 rows 9 times, ending by working Row 15. ***Always start the first of these 15 rows on right side of work***.

FRINGE

Follow Single Knot Fringe Instructions on page 16. Cut necessary strands 16″ in length in all colors. Working across the long end of afghan where partial fringe has already been made, using 1 strand, make a knot at every color change twice where there is no fringe; and once at the area where there is already a self-made fringe.

FISHERMAN

Fringe-as-you-go speeds the work on this sculptured beauty; there are no ends to weave in, no separate fringe to make.

SIZE

42" × 68"

MATERIALS

Mohair type worsted weight yarn: CARON
  DAZZLEAIRE:
    30 oz Off White #2615
Size J aluminum crochet hook (or size required for gauge)

GAUGE

11 sc = 4"; 3 rows = 1"

NOTES

This is an unusual afghan—you make the fringe as you work, by leaving a 7" end of yarn at the beginning and end of each row. **The afghan is worked entirely from the front side**, so be sure never to turn the work. Here are some techniques you will want to refer to as you work:

1. All sc stitches are worked in the **back loop only of each** stitch. This is the loop **away** from you.
2. All dc stitches are worked in the **front loop** of the sc stitch in the **second row below.**
3. From Row 2 on, begin every row like this: Leaving a 7" end of yarn, make a slip knot on hook; remove hook, insert it in **first st of previous row**, put slip knot back on hook and pull loop through, ch 1. **This counts as first st of the row.** This method gives a firm selvage edge.
4. **To end each row**, after working last st, cut yarn 7" from hook, pull yarn end through loop.
   Remember that each row is worked from the front; and that the yarn is begun and ended anew each row.

INSTRUCTIONS

Make a slip knot on hook, leaving a 7" end; ch 167 loosely.

Row 1: Sc in 2nd ch from hook and in each ch across; fasten off, leaving a 7" end. You should have 166 sc.

Rows 2 and 3: Join yarn in first st (Note 3 above); sc in **back loop only** of each st across; end off yarn

(Note 4 above). *Joining and ending methods will not be mentioned again*.

Row 4: Join yarn in first sc, sc in next 7 sc; sk next sc, work dc in front loop of sc 2 rows below: * sc in next 9 sc; sk next sc, dc as before in 2nd row below; repeat from * across to last 7 sc, sk next sc, dc as before in 2nd row below, sc in last 7 sc; there should be 16 dc across row.

Row 5: Join yarn in first sc, sc in next 6 sc, sk next sc, dc as before; sc, sk 1 sc, dc as before; * 7 sc, sk next sc, dc as before, sc, sk next sc, dc as before; repeat from * across to last 9 sts; sk next sc, dc as before, sc, sk next sc, dc as before, 6 sc; there should be 32 dc across row.

NOTE

From now on, remember to work each dc in front loop of sc 2 rows below; this will not be mentioned again.

Row 6: Join yarn in first sc, sc in next 5 sc, sk next sc, dc; 3 sc, sk next sc, dc; * 5 sc, sk next sc, dc; 1 sc, sk next sc, dc; rep from * across to last 10 sts, sk next sc, dc, 3 sc, sk next sc, dc, 5 sc.

Row 7: Join yarn in first sc; sc in next 4 sc, sk next sc, dc; 5 sc, sk 1 sc, dc; * 3 sc, sk next sc, dc, 5 sc; sk next sc, dc; repeat from * across to last 11 sts, sk next sc, dc, 5 sc, sk next sc, dc, 4 sc.

Row 8: Join yarn in first sc; sc in next 3 sc, sk next sc, dc; 7 sc, sk next sc, dc; * sc, sk next sc, dc; 7 sc, sk next sc, dc; repeat from * to last 12 sts, sk next sc, dc, 7 sc, sk next sc, dc, 3 sc.

Row 9: Join yarn in first sc; sc in next 2 sc, sk next sc, dc; *9 sc, sk next sc, dc; repeat from * across to last 13 sts, sk next sc, dc, 9 sc, sk next sc, dc, 2 sc.

Repeat Rows 4–9, 17 more times.

Repeat Row 2, twice. Fasten off.

With *wrong* side of afghan facing and working over the row just completed, attach yarn; ch 1, work 1 sc in each stitch across that end of afghan. Fasten off.

With *right* side of afghan facing and working over chain row, attach yarn, ch 1, sc in each ch across. Fasten off. Weave in all yarn ends, trim fringe evenly.

GOLDEN PLAID

Here's another quickest-of-the-quick! First you make a crochet mesh background, then "weave" doubled yarn through the mesh to create the plaid effect. Fun, fast, and easy!

SIZE

38″ × 57″

MATERIALS

Worsted weight yarn:
 16 oz each of:
  Yellow
  Gold
  Dark Gold
Size J aluminum crochet hook (or size required for gauge)

GAUGE

5 (dc, ch 1) = 3″; 6 rows = 3½″

NOTE
Afghan is worked in two stages. First the mesh background is crocheted; then the vertical rows of chain stitches are worked.

INSTRUCTIONS

With Gold and J hook, ch 138 loosely.

Foundation Row (right side): Dc in 6th ch from hook, * ch 1, skip 1 ch, dc into next ch; rep from * across, ch 4, turn. You should have 66 ch-1 spaces.

Pattern Row: Skip first dc and ch-1 sp; * dc in next dc, ch 1, sk ch-1 sp; repeat from * ending dc into 3rd ch of turning ch. Work two more Pattern Rows in Gold.

Continue to repeat Pattern Row in following color sequence: 2 rows Dark Gold, 4 rows Gold, until piece measures about 57″ long. Finish off, weave in all loose yarn ends.

WEAVING

Now you watch your afghan magically turn into a plaid as you "weave" yarn through the mesh spaces. These vertical (lengthwise) stripes are worked with the size K crochet hook, and *two strands of yarn*. Work in this color sequence:

> * 2 rows Gold
> 1 row Dark Gold
> 4 rows Yellow
> 1 row Gold

Repeat color sequence from * across the afghan, ending with 2 rows of Gold.

Start with right side of work facing you. Make a slip knot on K hook using 2 strands of yarn, and leaving about 8″ of yarn ends before the knot to be used as fringe.

Keeping yarn beneath work, begin at lower edge (along foundation chain) of first vertical row of ch-1 spaces and work a sl st in each ch-1 space to top of afghan. *To work sl st: Insert hook in ch-1 sp from front to back, hook 2 strands of yarn from beneath work and draw through work and loop on hook: sl st made.*

Be sure to work sl sts very loosely so as not to pucker or distort afghan. Finish off, leaving 8″ yarn ends as fringe.

Continue weaving in this manner across afghan, using color sequence as above. Trim fringe evenly.

EMERALD ISLE

The greens of Ireland inspired this beautiful afghan. If you can't find an ombre in all green, substitute one in greens with white. The open pattern is easy and fast.

SIZE

44" × 60" before fringing

MATERIALS

Worsted weight yarn:
    20 oz Shaded Green ombre
     8 oz Emerald Green
Size H aluminum crochet hook (or size required for gauge)

GAUGE

(3 dc + 1 ch-1 sp) = 1"; 4 rows dc = 2½"

NOTE

To change colors, YO, draw up a loop in last st (3 loops on hook), YO, draw through 2 loops; change to new color, YO, draw through remaining 2 loops.

INSTRUCTIONS

With ombre yarn, ch 134 loosely.

Row 1: Dc in 4th ch from hook and in next ch, ch 1; * dc in next 3 chs, ch 1; rep from * across to last 3 chs, dc in last 3 chs, ch 3, turn.

Row 2: Dc in first ch-1 sp; * ch 3, dc in next ch-1 sp; rep from * across, ending ch 3, dc in top of turning ch; ch 3, turn.

Row 3: 2 dc in first ch-3 sp; * ch 1, 3 dc in next ch-3 sp; rep from * across; ch 3, turn.

Repeat Rows 2 and 3, five times; then repeat Row 2 once, joining Emerald green in last st. You should have 12 rows of ombre; ch 3, turn.

Row 13: With Emerald, repeat Row 3.

Row 14: Dc in next 2 dc; * ch 1, dc in next 3 dc; rep from * across, ch 3, turn.

Rows 15 and 16: Repeat Row 14. At last st on Row 16, join ombre yarn, end off Emerald.

Rows 17–29: Repeat Rows 2 and 3 six times, then Row 2 once more.

Rows 30–33: Repeat Rows 13–16.

Repeat Rows 17–33, four times; repeat Rows 17–20, once more. Fasten off, weave in all loose ends.

BORDER

Row 1: Working on one long edge of afghan, join Emerald yarn at corner, ch 1, 2 sc in side of dc; * 2 sc in ch-3 sp, sc around dc; repeat from * across ombre rows; on solid rows, ** sc around dc, ch 1, rep from ** across solid rows; continue in this manner across edge to top corner, ending by working 2 sc in last ch-3 sp; ch 1, turn.

Row 2: Sc in each sc and ch-1 sp across row, fasten off. Work same border on other long edge.

FRINGE

Follow Single Knot Fringe Instructions on page 16. Cut 180 strands, 16" long using Emerald. Use 4 strands, folded in half, for each knot and tie knot at the ch-1 space across each short end of afghan (45 knots each side).

LILAC TIME

Pretty picots between double crochet shells add a lacey look to this lovely afghan made in a soft, fluffy yarn. Made on a size K hook to crochet in a jiffy.

SIZE

41" × 54" before fringing

MATERIALS

Mohair type worsted weight yarn, CARON DAZZLEAIRE:
   27 oz Lavender Mist #2656
Size K aluminum crochet hook (or size required for gauge)

GAUGE

2 dc and 2 picots = 3"; 2 rows = 1"

INSTRUCTIONS

Chain 118 sts LOOSELY.

Row 1 (wrong side): Work one sc in 6th chain from hook, * ch 3, 1 sc in 1st st of ch-3 (Picot made); sc into next chain, ch 2, skip 2 chs, sc into next chain. Repeat from * across, ch 3, turn.

Row 2: Ch 3, 2 dc into ch-2 space of previous row, * ch 2, 3 dc into next ch-2 space; rep from * across, chain 3, turn.

Row 3: * Work (sc, picot, sc) in next ch-2 space, ch 2; rep from * across, ending with 1 sc after 2nd last dc of previous row; ch 3, turn: Rep Rows 2 and 3 until piece measures approx 54", ending by working Row 3. Weave in all loose ends.

FRINGE

Follow Single Knot Fringe Instructions on page 16. Cut 174 strands for each side, 16" long. Use 6 strands, folded in half, for each knot fringe and tie knot around the ch-3 bars across each short end of afghan: 29 knots.

Trim fringe evenly.

QUICK KNITS

Knitting is so relaxing, even when your fingers fly quickly through these afghan patterns. Many are knitted with two strands of yarn, all on nice fat needles. Patterns range from lace designs to fisherman cables, from chunky stitches to smooth Stockinette Stitch.

Happy knitting!

FUCHSIA BLOSSOMS

This pretty pastel afghan combines two colors with two patterns: panels of stockinette stitch with panels of lacey, open stitches. It's lightweight and soft, a pleasure to knit and to use.

SIZE

46″ × 58″ before fringing

MATERIALS

Mohair type worsted weight yarn, CARON DAZZLEAIRE:
    12 oz Raspberry Punch Color A
    12 oz Azalea Color B
36″ long size 11 circular needle (or size required for gauge)

GAUGE

In Stockinette Stitch (K 1 row, P 1 row): 3 sts = 1″

NOTE

Circular needle is used to accommodate large number of stitches; do not join; turn work at end of each row.

INSTRUCTIONS

With Color A, cast on 158 sts loosely.

Row 1 (right side): * K 1, P 1; rep from * across row.

Row 2: * P 1, K 1; rep from * across row.
These two rows create a Seed Stitch pattern.

Rows 3–10: Repeat Rows 1 and 2, 4 times.

** Row 11: Knit.

Row 12: Purl.
These two rows create a Stockinette Stitch pattern.

Rows 13–26: Repeat Rows 11 and 12,

Row 27: Knit. Fasten off Color A.

LACE PATTERN

Join Color B.

Row 1 (wrong side): Purl.

Row 2: K1, * YO, sl 1, K1, PSSO, P2; repeat from * across ending K1.

Row 3: K3, * P1, K3; repeat from * across ending with P1, K2.

Row 4: K1, P1; * YO, sl 1, K1, PSSO, P2; repeat from * across ending last repeat with P1, K1.

Row 5: K2, * P1, K3; repeat from * across, ending last repeat with K3.

Row 6: K1, P2; * YO, sl 1, K1, PSSO, P2; repeat from * across ending with YO, sl 1, K1, PSSO, K1.

Row 7: K1, * P1, K3; repeat from * across ending K1.

Row 8: K1, P3, * YO, sl 1, K1, PSSO, P2; repeat from * across ending YO, sl 1, K1, PSSO.

Row 9: K4, * P1, K3; repeat from * across ending P1, K5.

Repeat Rows 2–9, 2 more times for pattern. ** Repeat between **'s 3 more times.

Work in Stockinette Stitch pattern for 17 rows.
Work in Seed Stitch pattern for 10 rows.
Bind off loosely in Seed Stitch.

FRINGE

Follow Single Knot Fringe Instructions on page 16. Cut strands, in both colors, 16″ long, and use 2 strands folded in half for each knot. Knot through EVERY OTHER stitch across each short end of afghan. (9 knots for Color A panel and 10 knots for Color B panel) Repeat for other side.

DAFFODIL

Fresh as a woods full of daffodils in spring, this afghan is made up of panels in an easy lace pattern, separated by garter stitch rows which add texture. Made on a size 10½ needle, it is an easy and quick project.

SIZE

41" × 53" before fringing

MATERIALS

Worsted weight yarn:
   21 oz Yellow
36" long size 10½ circular needle (or size required for gauge)
14 stitch markers

GAUGE

In Lace Pattern, 16 sts = 4½"

NOTES
1. Circular needle is used to accommodate large number of stitches; do not join, work back and forth in rows.
2. For ease in establishing the lace panels and the garter stitch panels, we suggest placing markers on the first row. Slip these markers as you work each following row. Markers may be removed when pattern is clearly established.

INSTRUCTIONS

Cast on 152 sts; knit 2 rows for border

Row 1: K8, place marker; * K2 tog, K2; YO, K5, YO; K2, sl 1 as if to knit, K1, PSSO; K3, place marker, K4, place marker.
Repeat from * across to last 8 sts, place marker, K8.

Row 2: K8, slip marker, * P16, slip marker, K4.
Repeat from * to last marker, K8.
Continue to slip markers on following rows.

Row 3: K8, * K5, K2 tog, K2; YO, K1, YO, K2; sl 1, K1, PSSO, K2, K4.
Repeat from * to last marker, K8.

Row 4: Repeat Row 2.

Row 5: K8, * K4, K2 tog; K2, YO, K3, YO, K2; sl 1, K1, PSSO; K1, K4.
Repeat from * to last marker, K8.

Row 6: Repeat Row 2.

Row 7: K8, * K3, K2 tog; K2, YO, K5, YO, K2; sl 1, K1, PSSO; K4.
Repeat from * to last marker, K8.

Row 8: Repeat Row 2.

Row 9: K8, * K2, K2 tog, K2; YO, K1, YO, K2; sl 1, K1, PSSO; K5, K4.
Repeat from * to last marker, K8.

Row 10: Repeat Row 2.

Row 11: K8, * K1, K2 tog, K2; YO, K3, YO, K2; sl 1, K1, PSSO; K8.
Repeat from * to last marker, K8.

Row 12: Repeat Row 2.
Repeat these 12 rows for pattern. Work until piece measures approx 53", ending by working Row 11. Knit 2 more rows. Bind off loosely in knit.

FRINGE

Follow Single Knot Fringe Instructions on page 16. Cut strands 16" long, and use 2 strands folded in half for each knot. Tie knot through each stitch across each short end of afghan.

Braid yarn from first 3 knots together loosely, knot firmly to fasten, leaving 1" ends. Continue braiding across. Trim ends.

BRIGHT WAVES

The beautiful yarn makes this afghan very special; try the interesting drop stitch pattern in a solid color, too. The lacey look is easy to do.

SIZE

48″ × 52″ before fringing

MATERIALS

Mohair type worsted weight yarn, CARON
 DAZZLEAIRE:
  18 oz Earthglow #2652
36″ long size 10½ circular needle (or size required
 for gauge)

GAUGE

In pattern, 21 sts = 7″; 8 rows = 3″

NOTE

Circular needle is used to accommodate large number of stitches; do not join, work back and forth in rows.

INSTRUCTIONS

Cast on 143 sts

Row 1: Knit.

Row 2: Knit.

Row 3: K3, * wind yarn twice around needle (abbreviated Y2RN); K1, Y2RN; K1, Y2RN; K5; repeat from * to end.

Row 4: K1, * K4; (drop yarn wound around needle, K1) 3 times; repeat from * to last 2 sts, K2.

Row 5: Knit.

Row 6: Knit.

Row 7: K1, Y2RN; * K5, Y2RN; K1, Y2RN; K1, Y2RN; repeat from * to last 2 sts, K2.

Row 8: K2; * (drop yarn wound around needle, K1) 3 times, K4; repeat from * to last st. Drop yarn wound around needle, K1.

Repeat these 8 rows for pattern until afghan measures approx 54″, ending by working Row 2. Bind off loosely.

FRINGE

Follow Single Knot Fringe Instructions on page 16. Cut strands 16″ long, and use 2 strands doubled for each knot. Tie knot in every other stitch at the short ends of afghan.

BLUE RHAPSODY

This lovely, chunky afghan is warmer than toast, and fast to make, too. It is knitted with two strands of yarn on big Size 17 needles.

SIZE

40" × 54"

MATERIALS

Mohair type knitting worsted weight yarn, CARON DAZZELAIRE:

    15 oz Slate Blue #2812 Color A
    30 oz Off White #2615 Color B

36" long size 17 circular needles (or size required for gauge)
Two stitch markers

GAUGE

With 2 strands of yarn, 6½ sts = 2"

NOTES

1. Circular needle is used to accommodate large number of stitches; do not join, work back and forth in rows.
2. Afghan is worked with two strands of yarn throughout.

PATTERN STITCH

Row 1 (right side): K 1; * with yarn in **back**, sl 1 as to purl, K 1; rep from * across, ending K 1.

Row 2: K 1; * with yarn in **front**, sl 1 as to purl, K 1; rep from * across, ending K 1.

Rows 3 and 4: Knit.
These four rows comprise one pattern.

INSTRUCTIONS

With Color B, cast on 129 sts.
Work 5 patterns of Color B
    3 patterns of Color A
    4 patterns of Color B
    3 patterns of Color A
Repeat above sequence 2 more times.
End 5 patterns of Color B.
Bind off loosely.

FRINGE

Follow Single Knot Fringe Instructions on page 16. Using Color B, cut strands 16" long, and use 2 strands folded in half for each knot. Tie knot through every other stitch across each short end of afghan.

SEDONA ROCKS

The beautiful colors of the yarns used in this afghan remind us of the magnificent colored rock formations around Sedona, Arizona. And the afghan would make a perfect cover for a cool Arizona evening.

SIZE

40" × 54"

MATERIALS

Mohair type knitting worsted weight yarn, CARON DAZZLEAIRE:
    12 oz Navajo ombre #2618 Color A
    18 oz Cinnamon #2824 Color B
36" long size 10½ circular needle (or size required for gauge)
Two stitch markers
Safety pin

GAUGE

In Garter Stitch (knit every row): 3 sts = 1"

NOTES

1. Circular needle is used to accommodate large number of stitches; do not join, work back and forth in rows.
2. There is a Garter Stitch border of 6 sts on each side of the afghan. Markers are used to set off these stitches; move markers on each row.

INSTRUCTIONS

With Color A, cast on 120 sts and knit 12 rows. Mark last row with safety pin to indicate wrong side of afghan. Fasten off Color A, join Color B.

Row 1: K 6, place marker on right needle; knit across to last 6 sts, place marker on right needle, K 6.

Row 2: K 6, sl marker; purl across to marker, sl marker, K 6.

NOTE

Sl markers on every following row; this will not be mentioned again.

Row 3 (right side): K 6, purl to last 6 sts, K 6.

Row 4: K 6; * K 1; (K 1, P 1, K 1) all in next st; rep from * across to last 6 sts, K 6.

Row 5: K 6; * K 3, P 1; rep from * across to last 6 sts, K 6.

Row 6: K 6; * K 1, P 3 tog; rep from * across to last 6 sts, K 6.

Row 7: K 6; purl to last 6 sts, K 6.

Row 8: K 6; * (K 1, P 1, K 1) all in next st, K 1; rep from * to last 6 sts, K 6.

Row 9: K 6; * P 1, K 3; rep from * across to last 6 sts, K 6.

Row 10: K 6; * P 3 tog, K 1; rep from * across to last 6 sts, K 6.

Rows 11–14: Rep Rows 3–6, ending on right side ** Repeat Rows 3–14 one more time, then repeat Rows 3–10 once (a total of 30 rows). Fasten off Color B, join Color A. Work in Garter Stitch for 11 rows, ending on wrong side; fasten off color A, attach Color B.

Repeat Rows 3–14 twice, then repeat Rows 3–10 once. Fasten off Color B, attach Color A.

Work in Garter Stitch for 11 rows, ending on wrong side. Fasten off Color A, attach Color B **

Repeat Rows 3–10, twice. Then work in Garter Stitch for 11 rows, ending on wrong side.

Repeat from ** to ** once, then work one more knit row. Bind off loosely as to knit.

SAMPLER STRIPES

You can make this beautiful afghan, and learn lots of new stitches at the same time! Don't be put off by the length of the pattern; each pattern stripe is really easy to make on Size 10 needles. Change the stripe colors as you desire to fit your own color scheme.

SIZE

46″ × 64″

MATERIALS

COATS & CLARK RED HEART® 4-ply handknitting
  yarn, Art. E. 267:
    12 oz each of:
      Coffee #365
      Orange #245
      Tangerine #253
      White #1
36″ long Size 10 circular needle (or size required
  for gauge)
10″ long Size 10 straight needles (or size required
  for gauge)
2 small stitch holders (or large safety pins)

GAUGE

In stockinette stitch (K 1 row, P 1 row): 4 sts = 1″
                                          6 rows = 1″

NOTE
A circular needle is used to accommodate large number of stitches;
do not join, work back and forth in rows.

INSTRUCTIONS

With circular needle and Coffee, cast on 208 sts loosely. Work in Garter Stitch (knit each row) for 18 rows. Fasten off Coffee. Place first 8 sts and last 8 sts on stitch holders to be worked later for borders.

FIRST PATTERN STRIPE

Attach Orange.

Row 1: * P 1, K 15; repeat from * across.
Row 2: * P 14, K 2; repeat from * across.
Hereafter always repeat from * across row.
Row 3: * P 3, K 13.
Row 4: * P 12, K 4.
Row 5: * P 5, K 11.
Row 6: * P 10, K 6.
Row 7: * P 7, K 9.

Row 8: * P 8, K 8.
Row 9: * P 9, K 7.
Row 10: * P 6, K 10.
Row 11: * P 11, K 5.
Row 12: * P 4, K 12.
Row 13: * P 13, K 3.
Row 14: * P 2, K 14.
Row 15: * P 15, K 1.
Row 16: Purl across; fasten off Orange.

SECOND PATTERN STRIPE

Attach White.

Row 1: Knit across.
Rows 2–8: * K 8, P 8.
Rows 9–16: * P 8, K 8.
Rows 17–24: * K 8, P 8; fasten off White.

THIRD PATTERN STRIPE

Attach Tangerine.

Row 1: K across.
Row 2: K 2, * P 12, K 4; end K 2.
Row 3: P 2, * K 12, P 4; end P 2.
Row 4: P 1, * K 2, P 10; K 2, P 2; end P 1.
Row 5: K 1, * P 2, K 10; P 2, K 2; end K 1.
Row 6: P 2, * K 2, P 8; K 2, P 4; end P 2.
Row 7: K 2, * P 2, K 8, P 2, K 4; end K 2.
Row 8: P 3, * K 2, P 6; end P 3.
Row 9: K 3, * P 2, K 6; end K 3.
Row 10: P 4, * K 2, P 4, K 2, P 8; end P 4.
Row 11: K 4, * P 2, K 4, P 2, K 8; end K 4.
Row 12: P 5, * K 2, P 2, K 2, P 10; end P 5.
Row 13: K 5, * P 2, K 2, P 2, K 10; end k 5.
Row 14: P 6, * K 4, P 12; end p 6.
Row 15: K 6, * P 4, K 12; end k 6.
Row 16: Repeat Row 14.
Rows 17–29: Work back from Row 13 through Row 1 to complete Diamond Pattern. Fasten off Tangerine.

FOURTH PATTERN STRIPE

Attach Coffee.

Next Row: Purl.
Rows 1–4: * K 4, P 4.
Rows 5–8: * P 4, K 4.

Rows 9–32: Repeat Rows 1– three times. Fasten off Coffee.

FIFTH PATTERN STRIPE

Attach Orange.

Row 1: Knit.

Row 2: * K 2, P 6.

Row 3: * K 6, P 2.

Row 4: P 1, * K 2, P 6; end P 5.

Row 5: K 5, * P 2, K 6; end K 1.

Row 6: P 2, * K 2, P 6; end P 4.

Row 7: K 4, * P 2, K 6; end K 2.

Row 8: P 3, * K 2, P 6; end P 3.

Row 9: K 3, * P 2, K 6; end K 3.

Row 10: P 4, * K 2, P 6; end P 2.

Row 11: K 2, * P 2, K 6; end K 4.

Row 12: P 5, * K 2, P 6; end P 1.

Row 13: K 1, * P 2, K 6; end K 5.

Row 14: * P 6, K 2.

Row 15: * P 2, K 6.

Row 16: K 1, * P 6, K 2; end K 1.

Row 17: P 1, * K 6, P 2; end P 1.

Rows 18–31: Repeat Rows 2–15. Fasten off Orange.

SIXTH PATTERN STRIPE

Attach White.

Row 1: Purl.

Row 2: K 2, * P 8, K 4; end K 2.

Row 3: P 2, * K 8, P 4. end P 2.

Rows 4–9: Repeat Rows 2 and 3 alternately.

Row 10: Knit.

Row 11: Purl.

Row 12: P 4, * K 4, P 8; end P 4.

Row 13: K 4, * P 4, K 8; end K 4.

Rows 14–19: Repeat Rows 12 and 13 alternately.

Row 20: Knit.

Rows 21–40: Repeat Rows 1–20; Fasten off White.

SEVENTH PATTERN STRIPE

Attach Tangerine.

Row 1: Purl.

Row 2: P 11, * K 2, P 22; end K 2, P 11.

Row 3: K 11, * P 2, K 22; end P 2, K 11.

Row 4: P 10, * K 4, P 20; end K 4, P 10.

Row 5: K 10, * P 4, K 20; end P 4, K 10.

Row 6: P 9, * K 6, P 18; end K 6, P 9.

Row 7: K 9, * P 6, K 18; end P 6, K 9.

Row 8: P 8, * K 8, P 16; end K 8, P 8.

Row 9: K 8, * P 8, K 16; end P 8, K 8.

Row 10: P 7, * K 10, P 14; end K 10, P 7.

Row 11: K 7, * P 10, K 14; end P 10, K 7.

Row 12: P 6, * K 12, P 12; end K 12, P 6.

Row 13: K 6, * P 12, K 12; end P 12, K 6.

Row 14: P 5, * K 14, P 10; end K 14, P 5.

Row 15: K 5, * P 14, K 10; end P 14, K 5.

Row 16: P 4, * K 16, P 8; end K 16, P 4.

Row 17: K 4, * P 16, K 8; end P 16, K 4.

Row 18: P 3, * K 18, P 6; end K 18, P 3.

Row 19: K 3, * P 18, K 6; end P 18, K 3.

Row 20: P 2, * K 20, P 4; end K 20, P 2.

Row 21: K 2, * P 20, K 4; end P 20, K 2.

Row 22: P 1, * K 22, P 2; end K 22, P 1.

Row 23: K 1, * P 22, K 2; end P 22, K 1.

Row 24: Repeat Row 22.

Rows 25–44: Work back from Row 21 through Row to 2 to complete Diamond Pattern. Fasten off Tangerine.

EIGHTH PATTERN STRIPE THROUGH THIRTEENTH PATTERN STRIPE

Work Sixth (Rows 1–39), Fifth, Fourth, Third (Rows 1–28), Second and First Pattern Stripes. Fasten off Orange. Leave sts on needle to be worked later for border.

LEFT BORDER

Move the 8 border sts from holder to a straight needle, attach Coffee. Work in garter stitch until border measures same length as center section, ending at inner edge. Break off Coffee. Place sts on stitch holder.

RIGHT BORDER

Work as for left Border, ending at outer edge. ***Do not break off Coffee.***

TOP BORDER

K across sts of Right Border, Center Section and Left Border. Work in garter stitch for 17 rows. Bind off loosely.

Sew inner edge of right and left border in place.

EASY FEATHER AND FAN

This beautiful, traditional pattern stitch originated in the Scottish Shetland Islands, where the famous Shetland lace knit shawls were created. This was one of the most popular of the lace stitches. Our afghan works up quickly on size 11 needles, and is made in three panels. We made our model in an ombre yarn, but it would be just as pretty worked in a solid color.

SIZE

47″ × 60″

MATERIALS

Worsted weight yarn:
    28 oz Dusty Rose ombre
14″ long size 11 straight knitting needles (or size required for gauge)

GAUGE

In garter stitch (knit every row), 7 sts = 2″

NOTE

You should test your gauge by making a 4″ garter stitch square before starting on the afghan. If your gauge is not correct, you may not have enough yarn to complete the project.

INSTRUCTIONS

PANEL *(make 3)*

Cast on 54 sts.

Bottom Border: Knit six rows.

Pattern Stitch
Row 1 (right side): Knit.

Row 2: Purl.

Row 3: * (K 2 tog) 3 times; (YO, K 1) 6 times; (K 2 tog) 3 times; rep from * across row.

Row 4: Knit.

Repeat Rows 1 through 4 until piece measures about 59″ long, ending by working Row 2 of Pattern Stitch.

Top Border: Knit six rows. Bind off loosely.

FINISHING

With right sides facing, join two panels along edge with overcast stitch, taking care to match rows carefully. Do not pull yarn too tightly as you sew. Join third panel in same manner.

FISHERMAN CABLES AND LATTICE

Two kinds of cables as well as a beautiful lattice pattern make this afghan fun as well as quick. Knit it with two strands of yarn, and on big Size 11 needles.

SIZE

50″ × 66″ before fringing

MATERIALS

COATS & CLARK RED HEART® 4-ply handknitting yarn, Art. E. 267:
    64 oz of Eggshell #111
36″ long Size 11 circular needle (or size required for gauge)
Cable stitch holder or double-point needle

GAUGE

With 2 strands of yarn held together: 4 sts = 1″
                                    4 rows = 1″

NOTES

1. Work with 2 strands of yarn held together throughout.
2. Circular needle is used to accommodate large number of stitches; do not join; work back and forth in rows.

INSTRUCTIONS

SIDE PANEL (make 2)

Starting at narrow edge, with 2 strands held together, cast on 64 sts loosely.

Row 1: P 2, K 6, P 2, place a marker on needle; K 44, place a marker on needle; P 2, K 6, P 2.

Row 2: K 2, P 6, K 2, slip marker; purl to next marker, slip marker, K 2, P 6, K 2. **Always slip markers**.

Row 3: P 2, K 6, P 2; * skip next st; with yarn in front of left-hand point of needle, knit in front of next st **but do not slip off needle**, knit the skipped st, slip **both sts** off left-hand point of needle: Right Twist made; skip next st, knit in back of next st, knit the skipped st, slip both sts off left-hand point of needle: Left Twist made. Repeat from * to next marker, P 2, K 6, P 2.

Row 4: Repeat Row 2.

Row 5: P 2, slip next 3 sts onto dp needle and hold in front of work, K next 3 sts, K the 3 sts from dp needle: Cable Twist made; P 2, * make a Left Twist, make a Right Twist. Repeat from * to next marker, P 2, Cable Twist as before, P 2.

Row 6: Repeat Row 2. Repeat last 4 rows (Rows 3–6) for pattern. Work in pattern until length is 66 inches, ending by working a wrong-side row. Bind off loosely.

CENTER PANEL

Starting at narrow edge, with 2 strands held together, cast on 72 sts.

Row 1: P 3, K 6, (P 4, K 6) 6 times; P 3.

Row 2: K 3, P 6, * K 4, P 6. Repeat from * to last 3 sts, K 3.

Row 3: P 3, slip next 3 sts onto dp or cable needle and hold in back of work, K next 3 sts, K the 3 sts from dp needle: Right Cable Twist made; (P 4, Right Cable Twist) 6 times; P 3.

Row 4: Repeat Row 2.

Row 5: P 2, * slip next st onto dp needle and hold in back of work, K next 3 sts, P the st from dp needle: cable moved to the right; slip next 3 sts onto dp needle and hold in front of work, P next st, K the 3 sts from dp needle: cable moved to the left; P 2. Repeat from * across.

Row 6: K 2, * P 3, K 2. Repeat from * across.

Row 7: P 1, * move cable to right, P 2, move cable to left; repeat from * to last st, P 1.

Row 8: K 1, P 3, K 4, * P 6, K 4. Repeat from * to last 4 sts, P 3, K 1.

Row 9: P 1, K 3, P 4, slip next 3 sts onto dp needle and hold in front of work, K next 3 sts, K the 3 sts from dp needle—Left Cable Twist made; (P 4, Left Cable Twist) 5 times; P 4, K 3, P 1.

Row 10: Repeat Row 8.

Row 11: P 1, * move cable to left, P 2, move cable to right; repeat from * to last st, P 1.

Row 12: Repeat Row 6.

Row 13: P 2, move cable to left; * move cable to right, P 2, move cable to left; repeat from * to last 6 sts, move cable to right, P 2.

Row 14: Repeat Row 2. Repeat last 12 rows (Rows 3–14) for pattern. Work in pattern until length is same as side panel, ending by working a wrong-side row. Bind off loosely.

FINISHING

Pin panels out to measurements, dampen and let dry. Then sew panels together lengthwise, taking care to match rows. For fringe, follow Double Knot Fringe instructions on page 16. Cut strands each 26″ long, and use 6 strands in each knot. On each narrow edge of afghan, for Row 1 of fringe, make a knot at corner of each end; then make 49 more knots evenly spaced along same edge. Complete fringe as in instructions.

HORSESHOE CABLES

Double yarn and Size 15 needles make this fisherman afghan a quick one. Between the unusual Horseshoe Cables are panels of Cellular Stitch, adding interesting texture.

SIZE

59" × 64"

MATERIALS

COATS & CLARK RED HEART® 4-ply handknitting yarn, Art. E. 267:
    44 oz of Eggshell #111
36" long Size 15 circular needle (or size required for gauge)
Cable stitch holder or double-point needle

GAUGE

In Cellular Stitch (see Pattern Row 1) with two strands of yarn: 5 sts = 2½"
                13 rows = 4"

NOTES
1. Work with 2 strands of yarn held together throughout.
2. Circular needle is used to accommodate large number of stitches; do not join; work back and forth in rows.

INSTRUCTIONS

With 2 strands held together, cast on 120 sts. Do not join, *turn*.

Row 1 (wrong side): YO, sl 1, K 2 tog, PSSO; (YO, K 1, YO, sl 1, K 2 tog, PSSO) 6 times; YO, K 1, YO: Cellular Panel made; * place a marker on needle, P 1, place another marker on needle, K 2, P 12, K 2: Horseshoe Panel made; place a marker, P 1, place another marker, YO, sl 1, K 2 tog, PSSO; (YO, K 1, YO, sl 1, K 2 tog, PSSO) 6 times; YO, K 1, YO. Repeat from * once more.

NOTE
Be careful not to drop the YO at beg or end of row; each YO is worked as a st. Three cellular Panels and two Horseshoe Panels have been started.

Row 2: * P across to next marker, slip marker, K 1, slip marker, P 2, K 12, P 2, slip marker, K 1, slip marker; repeat from * once more; P remaining sts. *Always slip markers.*

Row 3: YO, K 2 tog; (YO, sl 1, K 2 tog, PSSO; YO, K 1) 6 times; YO, sl 1, K 2 tog, PSSO; * P 1, K 2, P 12, K 2, P 1, YO, K 2 tog; (YO, sl 1, K 2 tog, PSSO, YO, K 1) 6 times; YO, sl 1, K 2 tog, PSSO; repeat from * once more.

Row 4: Repeat Row 2.

Row 5: YO, sl 1, K 2 tog, PSSO; (YO, K 1, YO, sl 1, K 2 tog, PSSO) 6 times; YO, K 1, YO, * P 1, K 2, P 12, K 2, P 1, YO, sl 1, K 2 tog, PSSO; (YO, K 1, YO, sl 1, K 2 tog, PSSO) 6 times; YO, K 1, YO; repeat from * once more.

Row 6: * P across to next marker, K 1, P 2; slip next 3 sts onto dp needle and hold in back of work; K next 3 sts, K the 3 sts from dp needle, slip next 3 sts onto dp needle and hold in front of work; K next 3 sts, K the 3 sts from dp needle, P 2, K 1; repeat from * once more, purl remaining sts.

Row 7: Repeat Row 3.

Row 8: Repeat Row 2.

Row 9: Repeat Row 5. Repeat last 8 rows (Rows 2–9) for pattern. Work in pattern until afghan measures about 59 inches, ending with Row 9. Bind off.

Pin to measurements, dampen and leave to dry.

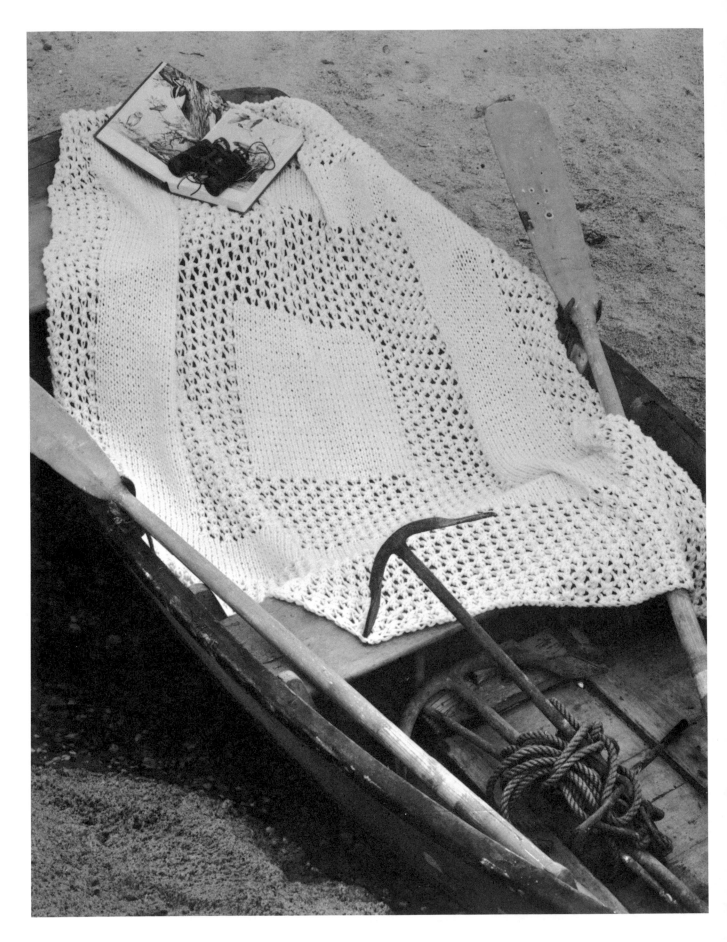

QUICK LACE

This beautiful, creamy lace afghan is made with two strands of yarn, on Size 15 needles—what could be faster? And you'll love the pretty, feminine look.

SIZE

47" × 75"

MATERIALS

COATS & CLARK RED HEART ® 4-ply handknitting yarn, Art. E. 267:
    52 oz Eggshell #111
36" long Size 15 circular needle (or size required for gauge)

GAUGE

In Stockinette St (K 1 row, P 1 row), with 2 strands of yarn held together: 5 sts = 2"
                4 rows = 1½"

NOTES
1. Work with 2 strands of yarn held together throughout.
2. Circular needle is used to accommodate large number of stitches; do not join; work back and forth in rows.

INSTRUCTIONS

Starting at narrow edge, with 2 strands held together, cast on 116 sts. Do not join, turn.

Row 1: YO, sl 1, K 2 tog, PSSO; * YO, K 1, YO, sl 1, K 2 tog, PSSO; repeat from * across to within last st, YO, K 1.

NOTE
Be careful not to drop the YO at beg of rows.

Row 2: YO, P across: 117 sts.

Row 3: YO, K 2 tog; * YO, sl 1, K 2 tog, PSSO, YO, K 1; repeat from * across, end with YO, sl 1, K 2 tog, PSSO: 116 sts.

Row 4: Purl across.

Rows 5–36: Repeat Rows 1–4, eight times.

Row 37: Work first and last 12 sts as on Row 1, knit center 92 sts.

Row 38: YO, purl across.

Row 39: YO, K 2 tog; (YO, sl 1, K 2 tog, PSSO, YO, K 1) twice; YO, K 2 tog, K to last 12 sts, work in pattern across last 12 sts.

Row 40: Purl across.

Rows 41–52: Repeat Rows 37–40, three more times.

Row 53: Work in pattern across first 12 sts, K 16; work in pattern across next 60 sts, K 16; work in pattern across last 12 sts.

Row 54: YO, purl across.

Row 55: Repeat Row 53.

Row 56: Purl across.

Rows 57–76: Repeat Rows 53–56, five more times.

Row 77: Work in pattern across first 12 sts, K 16; work in pattern across next 16 sts, K 28; work in pattern across next 16 sts, K 16; work in pattern across last 12 sts.

Row 78: YO, purl across.

Row 79: Repeat Row 77.

Row 80: Purl across.

Rows 81–124: Repeat Rows 77–80, eleven more times.

Rows 125–148: Repeat Rows 53–76.

Rows 149–164: Repeat Rows 37–52.

Rows 165–200: Repeat Rows 1–36. Bind off loosely.

MOCK FISHERMAN

If you've always wanted to make a beautiful fisherman knit afghan but were afraid to tackle all those elaborate cable stitches, this is the project for you! The pattern is an easy mock cable with only four rows, which works up quickly on size 11 needles. To handle the large number of stitches, a circular needle is used. A rich fringe provides the finishing touch.

SIZE

42" × 55" before fringing

MATERIALS

Worsted weight yarn:
    50 oz Off White
36" long Size 11 circular needle (or size required for gauge)

GAUGE

In garter stitch (knit every row), 7 sts = 2"

NOTE

Test gauge by making a 3" garter stitch square before starting on the afghan. If your gauge is not correct, you may not have enough yarn to complete the project.

NOTES

Special techniques for mock cable pattern. In the following Mock Cable pattern, there are two special techniques.

1. **In Row 1 of the pattern**, you will be told to: sl 1, K 2, PSSO the two knit stitches. To do this, first be sure the yarn is moved back to the position for knitting before you slip the stitch. To PSSO, insert tip of left needle into the slipped stitch, draw it over the two knitted stitches, over and off the top of the right-hand needle (**Fig 1**). This results in one stitch decreased.

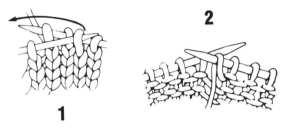

2. **In Row 2 of the pattern**, you will be told to: P 1, YO, P 1. To work this YO, bring the yarn back over the needle and completely around it to the front to again have yarn in the purl position (**Fig 2**). This results in one stitch increased.

MOCK CABLE PATTERN

Row 1 (right side): K 5, P 2; * sl 1, K 2, PSSO the two knit stitches; P 2; rep from * to last 5 sts, K 5.

Row 2: K 7; * P 1, YO, P 1; K 2; rep from * to last 5 sts, K 5.

Row 3: K 5, P 2; * K 3 (work the YO of previous row as a st), P 2; rep from * to last 5 sts, K 5.

Row 4: K 7; * P 3, K 2; rep from * to last 5 sts, K 5.

Repeat Rows 1 through 4 for pattern.

INSTRUCTIONS

Loosely cast on 157 sts; do not join, work back and forth in rows.

Bottom Border: Knit 2 rows. Now rep Rows 1 through 4 of Mock Cable pattern until piece measures 54½" long, ending by working Row 4 of pattern.

Top Border: Knit 2 rows. Bind off loosely. Weave in all loose yarn ends.

FRINGE

Follow Triple Knot Fringe instructions on page 16. Cut strands 22" long, and use 10 strands, folded in half, for each knot. Hold afghan with right side facing and one short edge at top. Working from left to right, make first knot in outer edge st of garter st side border, second knot in st of garter st side border; then work one knot below each cable across to other side. Work one knot in inner st of garter st side border, last knot in outer st of garter st side border.

BABY QUICKIES
TO KNIT & CROCHET

What fun it is to welcome a new baby with a hand-made gift. These beautiful afghans range from an elaborate Christening knitted blanket to a chunky striped crocheted afghan to lacey looks.

All are quick and all are easy.

[KNITTED]
LAVENDER LACE

Two shades of lavender stripe this perky mock cable afghan, worked on a size 11 needle.

SIZE

35″ × 38″

MATERIALS

Mohair type knitting worsted weight yarn, CARON DAZZLEAIRE:
  9 oz Lavender Mist #2656 Color A
  6 oz Crystal Lilac #2644 Color B
29″ size 11 circular needle (or size required for gauge)
2 stitch markers

GAUGE

In Garter Stitch (knit every row): 12 sts = 3″

NOTE
There are 12 sts of Garter Stitch border on each side of afghan; markers are used after the first 8 Garter Stitches and before the last 8 Garter Stitches for ease in working pattern; slip markers on each row.

INSTRUCTIONS

With Color A, cast on 116 sts loosely. Knit 12 rows. Cut Color A, join Color B.

PATTERN STITCH

Row 1 (wrong side): K 8, place marker on needle; K 1, * P 2, K 2; rep from * across, to last 11 sts, P 2, K 1; place marker on needle, K 8.

Row 2: K 8; P 1, * K 1, YO, K 1; P 2; rep from * to last 11 sts, K 1, YO, K 1, P 1; K 8.

Row 3: K 8; K 1, * P 3, K 2; rep from * to last 12 sts, P 3, K 1; K 8.

Row 4: K 8; P 1, * K 3, pass first K st over the next 2 K sts; P 2; rep from * to last 12 sts, K 3, pass first K st over next 2 K sts, P 1; K 8.

Repeat Rows 1–4, 3 times more (except on Row 1, sl markers rather than place them). Finish off Color B, join Color A.

Repeating Rows 1 through 4 for pattern, work in following color sequence:

  4 rows Color A
  4 rows Color B
  4 rows Color A
  4 rows Color B
  16 rows Color A
  4 rows Color B
  4 rows Color A
  4 rows Color B
  4 rows Color A
  16 rows Color B
  4 rows Color A
  4 rows Color B
  4 rows Color A
  4 rows Color B
  16 rows Color A
  4 rows Color B
  4 rows Color A
  4 rows Color B

With Color A, knit 12 rows. Bind off loosely; weave in all loose ends.

[CROCHETED]
PINK PETALS

This pretty pink confection is in an attractive V-Stitch, combined with double crochet.

SIZE

33" × 38"

MATERIALS

Mohair type worsted weight yarn CARON
    DAZZLEAIRE:
        15 oz Pink #2605
Size K aluminum crochet hook (or size required for gauge)

GAUGE

3 dc = 1"

INSTRUCTIONS

Chain 105 loosely.

Foundation Row: Dc in 4th ch from hook and in each ch across: 103 dc; ch 2, turn (counts as 1 dc).

Row 2: Skip 1st dc, dc in next dc and in each dc across, ending by making a dc under the ch-2 bar; ch 2, turn.

PATTERN

Row 1: Skip 1st dc, dc in next dc; (1 dc, ch 1, 1 dc) all in next dc: (V-St made); * skip 2 dc, (1 dc, ch 1, 1 dc) all in next dc: (V-st made); repeat from * across, end skip 1 dc, 1 dc in next dc, dc under the ch-2: (33 V-sts with 2 dc at each end); ch 2, turn.

Row 2: Skip first dc, dc in each st across row, (work 1 dc in each dc of each V-St and 1 dc in ch): 103 sts; ch 2, turn.

Row 3: Skip first dc, dc in next st, skip 1 st, V-St in next st; * skip 2 sts, V-St in next st; repeat from * across, end skip 1 dc, 1 dc in next dc, dc under the ch-2: (33 V-Sts with 2 dc at each end).

Repeat Pattern rows 2 and 3 until afghan measures 37", ending by working Row 2 of pattern. Repeat Row 2 once more. Fasten off. Weave in all loose ends.

BORDER

Work a Shell Stitch pattern along the short ends of afghan. With right side of work facing, attach yarn under dc bar; ch 1, work shell of (sc, hdc, dc, hdc, sc) in same space; * work another Shell around the ch-2 of the V-St row; repeat from * across edge, ending with a shell around the ch-2 of the dc row; fasten off.

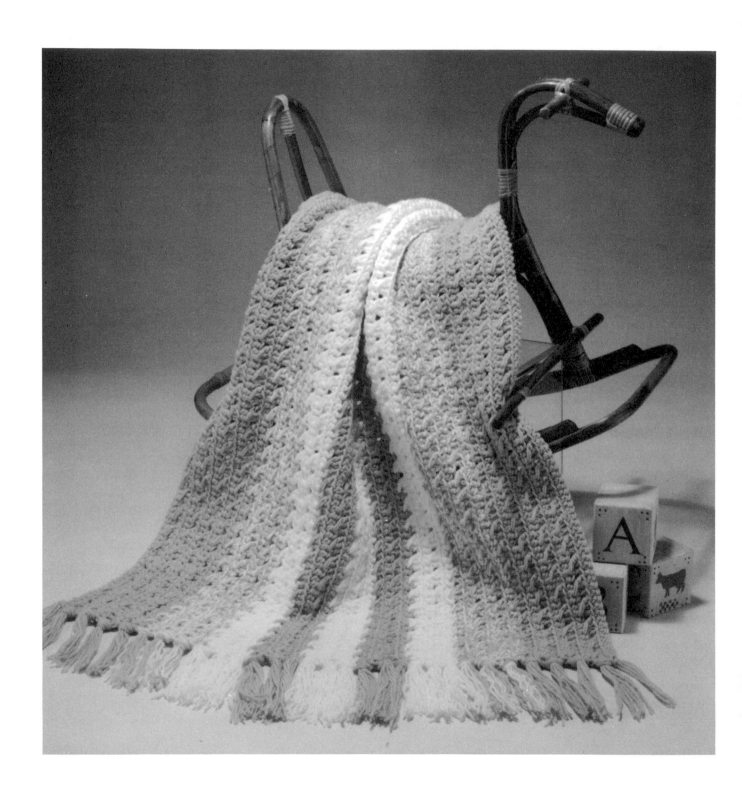

[CROCHETED]
STRIPES ON PARADE

Two yarn colors are combined for a three-color effect. The yarn is worked with two strands throughout, sometimes two of blue, sometimes two of white, sometimes one strand of each color. The stitch is an easy, fun to work cross stitch.

SIZE

32" × 38" before fringing

MATERIALS

Worsted weight yarn:
    22 oz White
    26 oz Blue
Size M wood crochet hook (or size required for gauge)

GAUGE

In pattern, 6 sts = 2¼"

NOTE

To change colors, draw up a loop in last st (2 loops on hook), change to new color, YO, draw through both loops. Cut off old color.

INSTRUCTIONS

Using 2 strands of Blue, ch 97 sts loosely.

Row 1: Skip 1st ch, sc in 2nd ch from hook and in each chain to end; ch 3, turn.

Row 2: Skip 1st sc, * 1 dc in each of next 2 sc, 1 dc in skipped sc (cross stitch made); skip next sc; repeat from * across ending 1 dc in last sc; ch 1, turn. You should have 31 cross stitches.

Row 3: Sc in each dc, ending sc in top of turning ch; ch 3, turn.

Rows 4–9: Repeat Rows 2 & 3, 3 more times. Change ONE of the strands of Blue to White on last stitch of Row 9.

Rows 10–15: Using one strand of blue and one of white, repeat Rows 2 and 3, 3 times, changing the one strand of Blue to White on the last stitch of Row 15.

Rows 16–19: Using 2 strands of White, repeat Rows 2 and 3, twice; changing to 2 strands of Blue on last stitch of Row 19.

Rows 20–23: Using 2 strands of Blue, repeat Rows 2 and 3, twice, changing to 2 strands of White on last stitch of row 23.

Rows 24–27: Repeat Rows 16–19 (2 strands White).

Rows 28–31: Repeat rows 20–23 (2 strands blue).

Rows 32–35: Repeat rows 16–19 (2 strands white).

Rows 36–41: Repeat rows 10–15 (1 strand of each color).

Rows 42–49: Repeat rows 2–9 (2 strands blue); at end of **Row 49**, finish off, weave in all loose ends.

FRINGE

Follow Single Knot Fringe Instructions on page 16. Cut strands of each color 16" long. Working across each short end, use 6 folded strands of Blue, and tie a knot around the ch-3 bar of Row 2. Repeat across, matching solid color knots and mixed color knots & afghan.

[KNITTED]
SPRING GREEN

Mint green and ecru yarns are combined for a fresh, springtime look. The easy 4-row pattern uses slipped stitches to create a checkered effect.

SIZE

32″ × 36″

MATERIALS

Worsted weight mohair type yarn, CARON DAZZLEAIRE:
>   9 oz Frosty Mint #2643 Color A
>   6 oz Off White #2615 Color B
2 stitch markers
14″ size 11 straight needles (or size required for gauge)

GAUGE

7 sts = 2″; 9 rows = 2″

NOTES

1. Afghan has a 7-st Seed Stitch border on each side; markers are placed on Row 1 after the 7th st and before the last 7 sts for ease in following pattern. Slip markers on all following rows.
2. Pattern is worked alternately in two rows of each color; do not cut yarn not in use; carry loosely up side of work.

INSTRUCTIONS

With Color A, cast on 113 sts loosely.

BOTTOM BORDER

Row 1: * K 1, P 1; rep from * across row ending K 1. Repeat this row until border measures 2″; do not cut A.

PATTERN ROWS

Row 1: With Color B, (K 1, P 1) 3 times, K 1, place a marker on right needle to indicate end of Seed St side border; K 2, * with yarn in **back** of work, sl 1 as to purl, K 2; rep from * to last 9 sts, K 2; place a marker on right needle to indicate beginning of Seed St side border; work in Seed St across last 7 sts.

Row 2: Seed over 7 sts; P 2, * with yarn in **front**, slip 1 st as to purl, P 2; Repeat from * to marker, Seed over last 7 sts. Drop Color B.

Row 3: With Color A, Seed over 7 sts; knit to last 7 sts, Seed over last 7 sts.

Row 4: Seed over 7 sts, purl to last 7 sts, Seed over last 7 sts.

Repeat Rows 1–4 until piece measures about 34″ from cast-on row, ending by working Row 2; cut off Color B.

TOP BORDER

With Color A, repeat Bottom Border Row 1 for 2″; bind off loosely in Seed St. Weave in all loose ends.

[CROCHETED]
IN THE PINK

Rows of cross stitches add texture interest to this feminine afghan designed to welcome a precious little girl.

SIZE

32″ × 36″

MATERIALS

Mohair type worsted weight yarn, CARON DAZZLEAIRE:
    15 oz Pink #2605
Size J aluminum crochet hook (or size required for gauge)

GAUGE

3 dc = 1″

INSTRUCTIONS

Ch 110 loosely.

Row 1: Dc in 4th chain from hook and in each ch across; counting ch-3 as 1 dc, you should have 108 dc; ch 3, turn.

Row 2: Skip first dc, dc in each dc across, dc in top of ch-3; ch 3, turn.

Row 3: Repeat Row 2.

Row 4 (cross stitch row): Skip first 2 dc, dc in next dc, dc in skipped dc; * skip next dc, dc in next dc, dc in skipped dc; repeat from * across, ending dc in top of ch-3; ch 3, turn.

Rows 5–7: Repeat Row 4.

Rows 8 and 9: Repeat Row 2.

Repeat rows 2–9 until piece measures approx 36″; repeat Row 2 once more. Fasten off.

FRINGE

Follow Single Knot Fringe Instructions on page 16. Cut strands 16″ long, and use 2 strands folded for each knot. Tie knots around the ch-3 or dc bars across each short end of afghan.

[CROCHETED]
SWEET SHELLS

Two strands of yarn and a size N hook add up to a lickety-quick afghan. Pretty shell stitches in shades of ombre, white and lilac create the design.

SIZE

40" × 43"

MATERIALS

Worsted weight mohair type yarn, CARON
    DAZZLEAIRE:
        4 skeins White
        2 skeins Crystal Lilac
        4 skeins Wildflower Ombre
Size N crochet hook (or size required for gauge)

GAUGE

2 shells = 5½"

NOTE
Afghan is worked with 2 strands of yarn throughout.

INSTRUCTIONS

With one strand of ombre and one strand of white held together, ch 75.

Row 1: 4 dc in 4th ch from hook; * skip 2 ch, sc in next ch, sk 2 ch; 5 dc in next ch (shell made), rep from * across.

Row 2: Ch 3, turn; 2 dc in base of turning ch; * sc in top of next shell (top of center dc), shell of 5 dc in next sc; rep from * across, ending with 3 dc in last st.

Row 3: Ch 1, turn; sc in base of ch-1, * shell of 5 dc in next sc, sc in next shell, rep from * across.

Repeat Rows 2 and 3 for pattern until piece measures about 40" from starting ch. Finish off yarn, join 2 strands of Crystal Lilac in same st.

EDGING

Work Row 2 of pattern; at end of row, make 3 sc in corner st instead of 1 sc; continue to work Row 2 of pattern down side of afghan, again work 3 sc in corner; then across bottom of afghan, 3 sc in corner; then up opposite side, join. Now work Row 3 of pattern around all four sides, again working 3 sc in corner sts.

Finish off, weave in all yarn ends.

[KNITTED]
BLUE BOY

Seed stitch panels combined with chevrons make the design for this colorful afghan, worked with two strands of yarn on a size 15 needle. It would be just as pretty in yellow, pink, lavender or white.

SIZE

32″ × 36″ before fringing

MATERIALS

Mohair type worsted weight yarn, CARON DAZZLEAIRE:
    18 oz Sky Blue #2620
29″ size 15 circular needle (or size required for gauge)
8 stitch markers

GAUGE

18 sts = 7½″; 8 rows = 2½″

NOTES
1. Two strands of yarn are used throughout.
2. Markers are used to separate the Seed Stitch patterns from the Chevron Patterns for ease in working; sl markers on every row.

STITCH PATTERNS

SEED STITCH PATTERN

[worked over 7 sts]:
(K1, P1,) 3 times; K1.

CHEVRON PANEL PATTERN

[worked over 11 sts]:
Rows 1, 3, 5, 7: Purl (wrong side).
Row 2: K1, YO, Sl 1, K1, PSSO, K5, K2 tog, YO, K1.
Row 4: K2, YO, Sl 1, K1, PSSO, K3, K2 tog, YO, K2.
Row 6: K3, YO, Sl 1, K1, PSSO, K1, K2 tog, YO, K3.
Row 8: K4, YO, Sl 1, K2 tog, PSSO, YO, K4.

INSTRUCTIONS

With 2 strands of yarn cast on 79 sts; do not join; work back and forth in rows.

Row 1 (wrong side): Work in Seed St for 7 sts, * place marker on right needle; P 11 (Chevron Panel), place marker on right needle; work Seed St for 7 sts; repeat from * across row.

Row 2: Work in Seed St to marker; * move marker to right needle, work Row 2 of Chevron pattern, move marker, work in Seed St to marker; repeat from * across row.

Row 3: Repeat Row 1.

Row 4: Repeat Row 2, BUT work Row 4 of Chevron Panel pattern.

Row 5: Repeat Row 1.

Row 6: Repeat Row 2, BUT work Row 6 of Chevron Panel pattern.

Row 7: Repeat Row 1.

Row 8: Repeat Row 2, BUT work Row 8 of Chevron Panel pattern.

Repeat these 8 rows, until afghan measures approx 36″ ending by working Row 8.

Bind off loosely in pattern stitch.

FRINGE

Follow Single Knot Fringe Instructions on page 16. Cut strands 16″ long and use two strands doubled for each knot. Tie knot through every other cast-on or bound-off stitch across each short end of afghan.

[CROCHETED]
GINGHAM AND LACE

Granny squares create a gingham pattern in this afghan, edged with a lacey border and trimmed with a ribbon bow. A pretty design for a pretty baby.

SIZE

30″ × 44″

MATERIALS

Worsted weight yarn:
    8 oz Dark Raspberry
    12 oz Med Raspberry
    12 oz White
1½ yds ⅜″ wide satin ribbon
Size I aluminum crochet hook (or size required for gauge)

GAUGE

One square = 4½″

INSTRUCTIONS

GRANNY SQUARE (make 12 dk raspberry; 24 med raspberry; and 12 white)

Rnd 1: Ch 4, join with a sl st to form a ring; ch 3, 2 dc in ring; * ch 2, 3 dc in ring; rep from * twice, ch 2, join with a sl st to top of beg ch-3.

Rnd 2: Sl st in each of next 2 dc and into ch-2 corner sp; ch 3, work (2 dc, ch 2, 3 dc) in next ch-2 corner sp; * work (3 dc, ch 2, 3 dc) in next ch-2 corner sp; rep from * twice, join with a sl st in top of beg ch-3.

Rnd 3: Sl st in each of next 2 dc and into ch-2 corner sp; ch 3, work (3 dc, ch 2, 3 dc) in next ch-2 corner sp; * 3 dc between next two 3-dc groups, in next ch-2 corner sp work (3 dc, ch 2, 3 dc); rep from * twice, 3 dc between next two 3 dc groups; join with a sl st to top of beg ch-3.

Rnd 4: Work as for Rnd 3, working 3 dc between each 3-dc group on each side; at end finish off, weave in ends.

ASSEMBLING

Afghan has 8 rows, with 6 squares in each row. Every odd-numbered row contains squares as follows, from left to right: * white, med Raspberry; rep from * twice. Every even-numbered row contains squares as follows, from left to right: * med Raspberry, dk Raspberry, rep from * twice.

To join, hold 2 squares with right sides together. Carefully matching stitches, begin in ch st at corner and sew with over cast st in outer loops only, ending in first ch st at next corner. Join all squares for each row, then join rows in same manner.

EDGING

Hold afghan with right side facing you; join white with an sc in any outer corner ch-3 sp; work 2 more sc in sp; sc in each st and in each corner of each square around, join with a sl st to first sc.

Lace Row: Ch 4, dc in same sc; * (dc, ch 1, dc) all in next st; rep from * around, join to 3rd ch of beg ch-4. Finish off.

RIBBON TRIM

Make bow as in photo, attach securely to one corner.

[KNITTED]
HEIRLOOM CHRISTENING BLANKET

Deeply textured white fan shells add texture to this ribbon-trimmed blanket that's sure to be a family heirloom. It would be charming also in a pastel color.

SIZE

32″ × 34″

MATERIALS

Worsted weight yarn:
    18 oz White
29″ size 10 circular needle (or size required for gauge)
8¼ yds, ⅜″ wide picot-edge white satin ribbon

GAUGE

In garter stitch (knit every row): 4 sts = 1"

FAN SHELL PATTERN STITCH

Special Abbreviation used in Patt St: SSK (slip, slip, knit) = sl next 2 sts as to knit (one at a time) to right-hand needle (**Fig 1**), insert tip of left-hand needle through these 2 slipped sts on right-hand needle, then knit both sts tog in this position (**Fig 2**).

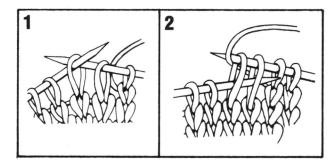

INSTRUCTIONS

Cast on 114 sts *loosely*. Do not join; work back and forth in rows. Knit 3 rows.

Now work in Fan Shell Patt St as follows:

Row 1 (right side): K1, K2 tog; YO (for eyelet at side edge—for weaving ribbon through later), K2, (YO, K1) 5 times; * YO, K4, (YO, K1) 5 times; rep from * to last 5 sts, YO, K2; YO (for eyelet at other side edge), K2 tog, K1.

NOTE
Throughout patt, each YO counts as one st.

Row 2: K3, P2, K 11; * P4, K 11; rep from * to last 5 sts, P2, K3.

Row 3: K5, P 11; * K4, P 11; rep from * to last 5 sts, K5.

Row 4: K3, * P2 tog, P 11, P 2 tog tbl (through back lps— see **Fig 3**): rep from * to last 3 sts, K3.

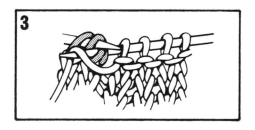

Row 5: K1, K2 tog, YO (for eyelet); * SSK (see **Figs 1 and 2**), K9, K2 tog; rep from * to last 3 sts, YO (for eyelet), K2 tog, K1.

Row 6: K3, * P2 tog, P7, P2 tog tbl; rep from * to last 3 sts, K3.

Row 7: K5, (YO, K1) 5 times; * YO, K4, (YO, K1) 5 times; rep from * to last 5 sts, YO, K5.

Row 8: Rep Row 2.

Row 9: K1, K2 tog; YO (for eyelet), K2, P 11; * K4, P 11; rep from * to last 5 sts, K2, YO (for eyelet), K2 tog, K1.

Row 10: Rep Row 4.

Row 11: K3, * SSK, K9, K2 tog; rep from * to last 3 sts, K3.

Row 12: Rep Row 6.
Rep Rows 1 through 12, 16 times more. Then rep Row 1 once more.

Next Row (wrong side): K3, K2 tog, K 11; * (K2 tog) twice, K 11; rep from * to last 5 sts, K2 tog, K3.

Next Row: K3, K2 tog, K9; * (K2 tog) twice, K9; rep from * to last 5 sts, K2 tog, K3.

Next Row: K3, K2 tog, K7; * (K2 tog) twice, K7; rep from * to last 5 sts, K2 tog, K3. Bind off *loosely* in knit. Weave in all ends.

RIBBON TRIM

First cut ribbon into 4 lengths: 2 lengths each 72" long and 2 lengths each 76" long. With right side of afghan facing you, first weave one 76" length through eyelets along one side edge of afghan, leaving equal lengths of ribbon at each end. Repeat at other side edge. Then start in same eyelet with side ribbon and weave 72" length through YO holes of Patt St along bottom edge of afghan, ending in same eyelet with other side ribbon and leaving equal lengths of ribbon at each end. Repeat at top edge. Tie a bow at each corner, leaving ends for streamers.

LEMON LACE & SUNSHINE GRANNY

[CROCHETED]
SUNSHINE GRANNY

For a young Merry Sunshine, this bright granny can be a crib cover-up or a play rug on the floor. Two shades of yellow, with white, provide the sunbeams.

SIZE

39″ × 50″

MATERIALS

Worsted weight yarn:
    14 oz White
    3½ oz Light Yellow
    7 oz Bright Yellow
Size H aluminum crochet hook (or size required for gauge)

GAUGE

Granny Square = 7″ × 7″

INSTRUCTIONS

Make 10 granny squares.
With light yellow ch 4, join with sl st to form ring.

Rnd 1: Ch 3 (count as 1 dc), work 2 dc in ring; * ch 1, work 3 dc in ring. Rep from * 2 times, ch 1; join with sl st into top ch of beg ch 3. Fasten off, leaving 3″ yarn end.

Rnd 2: With bright yellow, attach in ch 1 sp, ch 3 (count as 1 dc), work 2 dc into ch 1 sp; ch 2, work 3 dc in same ch 1 sp; * in next ch 1 sp, work 3 dc, ch 2, 3 dc, ch 1; rep from * 2 more times. Join with sl st into top ch of beg ch 3. Fasten off, leaving 3″ tail.

Rnd 3: With white attach in any ch 2 corner sp, ch 3 (count as 1 dc); As in Rnd 2, work corners as before, (3dc, ch 2, 3dc) in a ch 2 corner sp; Ch 1, 3 dc in each side ch 1 sp. End with ch 1, join with sl st into top ch of beg ch 3. **Do not fasten off**. Sl st across to ch 1 sp.

Rnds 4–6: Work as in rnd 3. Fasten off white after Rnd 6. Make 10 squares and sl st 6 together, two squares across and 3 squares down.

With light yellow, sl st in any ch 2 corner sp; ch 3 (count as 1 dc), 2 dc, ch 2, 3 dc in same corner sp; ch 1, 3 dc, ch 1 in next ch 1 sp. Continue in pattern around same as Rnd 3. End with sl st in top of beg ch 3. Work another round of light yellow. Fasten off. Continuing in same pattern, work 3 rows of bright yellow and 4 rows of white.

OUTSIDE BORDER (working on one side only)

Row 1: Attach bright yellow to any white corner sp, ch 3, work 2 dc in same sp; * Ch 1, 3 dc in next ch 1 sp; rep from * until next corner sp, ch 1, 3 dc in corner sp; Ch 4. Turn.

Row 2: 3 dc in first ch 1 sp; * Ch 1, 3 dc into next ch 1 sp; rep from * across row and into last ch 1 sp; Ch 1, dc into top of 3 dc. Ch 3, (count as 1 dc), turn.

Row 3: 2 dc into ch 1 sp; * ch 1, 3 dc into next ch 1 sp; rep from * across row, ending with ch 1, 1 dc into top of 3 dc of previous row. Fasten off.

Rows 4–5: Attach light yellow, rep rows 1 and 2. Fasten off.

Rows 6–10: Attach white and repeat rows 1 and 2 for 6 rows total. Fasten off.

Work remaining 3 sides in the same way. Sl st a granny square into each corner. Weave in all loose ends.

[KNITTED]
LEMON LACE

Easy and quick, this baby afghan has a lovely, light lacey look.

SIZE

36″ × 42″

MATERIALS

Worsted weight mohair type yarn, CARON
    DAZZLEAIRE:
        18 oz Light Yellow
14″ size 10 needles (or size required for gauge)

GAUGE

12 sts = 3″

INSTRUCTIONS

Cast on 144 sts loosely.

Row 1: Knit.

Row 2: Purl.

Row 3: K 1; * YO twice, K 1; rep from * across.

Row 4: * Sl 6 sts as to purl, dropping YO sts; this will form 6 long loops on right needle. With left needle, pick up the first group of 3 sts and pass first group over the second group of 3 sts. Now all 6 sts are on left needle; purl each of these 6 sts; rep from * across.

Row 5: Knit.

Row 6: Purl.

Rep these 6 rows until 32 pattern rows have been completed. Bind off loosely, weave in all yarn ends.

FRINGE

Following Single Knot Fringe instructions on page 16, cut strands into 14″ lengths; double strands and knot one strand into each st across short ends.

[CROCHETED]
PASTEL RAINBOW

A rainbow of soft pastels to wrap around the newest member of the family. The afghan is soft and light; baby will love it.

SIZE

35″ × 42″

MATERIALS

Mohair type worsted weight yarn, CARON
  DAZZLEAIRE:
    11 oz White
    7 oz Light Green
    7 oz Crystal Lilac
    7 oz Ombre
Size K aluminum crochet hook (or size required for
  gauge)

GAUGE

3 dc = 1″; 4 rows = 3″

INSTRUCTIONS

With White, loosely ch 99.

Row 1: Dc in 4th ch from hook and in next ch, (dc, ch 2, dc) in next ch; * dc in next ch, dec over next 3 chs as follows: (YO, draw up a lp in next ch, YO and draw through 2 lps on hook) 3 times, YO and draw through all 4 lps on hook: dec made; dc in next ch, (dc, ch 2, dc) in next ch; rep from * to last 3 chs, dc in next ch, dec over last 2 chs as follows: (YO, draw up a lp in next ch, YO and draw through 2 lps on hook) twice, YO and draw through all 3 lps on hook: dec made; ch 3, turn.

Row 2: Dc in each of next 2 dc; * (dc, ch 2, dc) in next ch-2 sp, dc in next dc, dec over next 3 sts, dc in next dc; rep from * to last ch-2 sp, (dc, ch 2, dc) in ch-2 sp, dc in next dc, dec over next 2 dc, leave ch-3 at end of row unworked; ch 3, turn.

Rep Row 2 four times more. At end of last row, change to Light Green in last st (pull new color through last 3 lps), cut White.

Rep Row 2 in the following color sequence:
    6 rows Light Green (just joined)
    6 rows Ombre
    6 rows Crystal Lilac
    6 rows White
    6 rows Light Green
    6 rows Ombre
    6 rows Crystal Lilac
    6 rows White
At end of last row, finish off and weave in all ends.

[CROCHETED]
LAVENDER DAISIES

The pretty flower-like stitch of this afghan combines with lovely, soft yarn to create a beautiful afghan for the new baby. Try it in other soft pastels, too, or in bright white.

SIZE

34" × 36"

MATERIALS

Mohair type worsted weight yarn, CARON DAZZLEAIRE:
  24 oz Lavender Mist #2656 Color A
  12 oz Crystal Lilac #2644 Color B
Size K and I aluminum crochet hooks

GAUGE

With K hook, 3 dc = 1"; 2 Daisy rows = 1½"

NOTE
To change color at end of row, work across, YO, draw up a loop in last st (3 loops on hook), YO, draw through 2 loops, change to new color; YO, draw through rem 2 loops, ch 3, turn.

INSTRUCTIONS

With Color A and K hook, ch 84 sts loosely.

Row 1: Dc in 4th ch from hook and in each ch across; ch 2, turn: 82 dc.

Row 2: Repeat Row 1, joining Color B on last st; ch 1, turn. Fasten off Color A.

Row 3: Sc in each dc across, ch 2, turn.

Row 4: Insert hook in 2nd ch from hook, YO, draw a loop through (2 loops on hook), insert hook in first sc, YO, draw a loop through; draw a loop through the next 2 sc, YO, draw loop through all 5 loops on hook, ch 1 (Daisy made); * insert hook in center loop of

Daisy just made, YO, draw a loop through; insert hook in last ch-1 of Daisy just made and pull loop through; draw a loop through next 2 sc, YO, draw a loop through all 5 loops, ch 1; repeat from * for pattern, ending by working a dc under turning ch: 40 Daisy patterns. Ch 1, turn.

Row 5: Skip first stitch, sc in next st and in each st across, ch 2, turn.

Row 6: Repeat Row 4.

Row 7: Repeat Row 5, changing to Color A in last stitch; fasten off Color B leaving a 4" yarn end for weaving later.

Row 8: With Color A, sk first sc, dc in next sc and in each st across; ch 2, turn.

Repeat Rows 2 through 8 for pattern, until afghan measures about 36", ending by working Row 2.

BORDER

Using size I hook:

Rnd 1: On right side with long end of afghan facing, attach Color A to corner of dc row. Work sc in each dc across to corner, work 3 sc in corner. Work sc in each dc bar to next dc corner (adjust sc sts to keep work flat). Work 3 sc in corner and in each dc to next corner; work 3 sc in corner and sc evenly spaced along side to beginning corner; slip stitch into sc at beg of round.

Rnd 2: Ch 1, sc in 1st sc and in each sc around, working 3 sc in each corner sc. Slip stitch in top of beg of rnd.

Rnd 3: Slip stitch to middle sc of next corner; sc, skip 2 sc; * (2 dc, ch 1, 2 dc, shell made) in next st; skip 2 sts, sc in next sc. Repeat from * to next corner, ending with a shell, sc in top of 3 sc group in corner. Fasten off.

Weave in all loose ends.

[CROCHETED]
PASTEL CAROUSEL

Lovely pastel shades create a new concept in afghans: a pinwheel circle! What a lovely shower gift this would make. It's fun and fast on a big size K hook.

SIZE

45″ diameter

MATERIALS

NOMIS EXCELLENCE worsted weight yarn, in 100 gr. skeins:
- 2 skeins White #301
- 2 skeins Baby Blue #304
- 2 skeins Yellow #307
- 2 skeins Baby Green #306
- 1 skein Pink #305

Size K aluminum crochet hook (or size required for gauge)

GAUGE

2 sc and 2 ch-1 sps = 1″; 3 rows = 1″

INSTRUCTIONS

Starting at center with White, loosely ch 71.

Row 1: Sc in 3rd ch from hook; * ch 1, sk 1 ch, sc in next ch; rep from * across row; you should have 35 sc and 34 ch-1 sps; ch 2, turn.

Row 2: Sk first sc, sc in next sp; * ch 1, sc in next sp; rep from * to last sc, ch 1, sc in sp under turning ch; ch 2, turn.

Row 3 (short row): Sc in first sp; * ch 1, sc in next sp; rep from * to last 3 sc, ch 1, sl st in next sp, leave last sp unworked; ch 1, turn.

Row 4: Sk first sl st and next sc, sc in next sp; * ch 1, sc in next sp; rep from * to last sc, ch 1, sc in sp under turning ch; ch 2, turn.

Row 5 (short row): Sc in first sp; * ch 1, sc in next sp; rep from * to last 2 sc of prev row, ch 1, sl st in next sp; ch 1, turn.

Rows 6 through 33: Rep Rows 4 and 5, 14 times more.

Row 34: Sk first sl st and next sc, sc in next sp, ch 1, sc in sp under turning ch; end at outer edge and draw Pink through 2 lps of last sc, cut White; ch 2, turn.

**Long Row: * Sc in first sp; * ch 1, sc in sp between next sc and sl st, ch 1, sc in next sp (where sl st was worked); rep from * to last 2 sc, ch 1, sc in next sp, ch 1, sc in sp under turning ch; you should now have 35 sc and 34 ch-1 sps; ch 1, turn.

Repeat Rows 2 through 34; end at outer edge and draw Baby Blue through 2 lps of last sc, cut old color; ch 2, turn. ******

Repeat from ** to ** in the following color sequence:
- Baby Blue (just joined)
- Yellow
- Baby Green
- White
- Pink
- Baby Blue
- Yellow
- Baby Green
- White
- Baby Blue

At end of last row, do not cut Baby Blue. You should have 12 color sections in all.

JOINING

Continuing with Baby Blue, crochet first and last sections together as follows: Hold sections with right sides together and carefully matching sps along Baby Blue edge with ch-1 sps along White edge, work instructions for Long Row, ending at center. Finish off, leaving 10″ end. Thread into tapestry or yarn needle and weave through sts around center opening, draw up tightly and fasten securely.

BORDER

Rnd 1: With right side facing you, join White in any outer edge st, work in sc evenly spaced around with ch 1 between each sc; ch 1, join with a sl st in beg sc; cut White, with Baby Green ch 1, do not turn.

Rnd 2: With Baby Green, sc in next sp; * ch 1, sc in next sp; rep from * around, ch 1, join with a sl st in beg sc; cut Baby Green, with White, ch 1, do not turn.

Rep Rnd 2 in each of the following colors:
- White (just joined)
- Yellow
- White
- Baby Blue
- White
- Pink
- White

At end of last rnd, finish off and weave in all loose ends. Lightly steam work flat.

143

INDEX